Designer Fashion Dolls

by Beauregard Houston-Montgomery

Published by

Hobby House Press, Inc.
Grantsville, MD 21536

DEDICATION

For My Father, Wil Stretch, who passed me the "collector" gene, (and always shows great tolerance for garden elves), and my late mother, Jenell, who introduced me (at infancy) to Chanel #5".

SPECIAL THANKS

Carolyn Cook & Ray Boileau, John Darcy Noble & Robert Clement, Benita Cassar Torreggiani & Kenny Aaronson, Tammy Blank, Theresa Black, Marlene Mura & Karen Caviale, Timothy & Karin Greenfield-Sanders, Karen Tina Harrisson, John Puzewski, Patti Lewis, Laura Meisner, Doug James, Cindy & Joey Adams, Wendy Goodman, Ryan Lance & Michael Torres, Tom Ford & Richard Buckley, Stanley & Irene Wahlberg, Margiann Flanagan, Maria Soma, Linda Ross, Lynn Yaeger, Michael Musto, the late Andy Warhol, John Carmen, Cathay Che, Brigid Berlin, Brigitte Deval, Ruth & Eliot Handler, David Sage, Mario Buatta, Colin Shanley, Ray Dowd, Janet Charleton, Roxanne Pulitzer, Brian & Sonia Goodfellow, Vivienne Westwood, Margaret Kufen, Diane Kapantzos, the late William Travilla, Suzanne O'Brien, Dallas Boesendahl, Mel Odom, Gabriela & Stefan Johansson, Harvey Rosenberg & Jennifer Anderson, Nick Grandee, Harry King & Orazio Fortunato, Alison Moore, Lisa Elliott Ellerby, Patricia Jacobs, Nolan Miller, Alvah Chin, Phyllis Belanger, Bradford Samuels, Juan Andres Ortiz & John Mckitterick, Chi Chi Valenti & Johnny Dynel, Betty Jane Haden, Cathy Cook, L. Edwards, David Croland, Diana Balton, Stacy Morrison, David Trinidad, Laurie Campbell, Elizabeth Racine, Leonard Abrams, Stephen Saban, Heidi, Cynthia, Natasha, and Ruben Bansie/Snellman, Charles & Yvette Elkain, Jason Carter, John Diamandis, Lois Lewis, the late Julian de Rothschild, the late Thelma Krause, Yla Eason & Menelik, Oleg Cassini & Dale, Alice Hudson, Shirley Baldwin King, Pito Collas, Jacob Getz, Ande' Whyland & Dani Johnson, Patrick McMullen, Suzanne Bartsch, Celebrity Service's Bill Murray, Bob Collacello, Oliver Rish, Sylvia Miles, Zohra Lampert, Pamela Tiffen, Quintin Crisp and Sydney Biddle Barrows Hoffman.

Additional copies of this book may be purchased at $14.95 (plus postage and handling) from

HOBBY HOUSE PRESS, INC.
1 Corporate Drive
Grantsville, Maryland 21536

1-800-554-1447
or from your favorite bookstore or dealer.

©1999 Beauregard Houston-Montgomery

ISBN: 0-87588-524-1

CONTENTS

FOREWORD

JOHN DARCY NOBLE

When I was asked to write this introduction, my first response was "Beauregard, you are my godson, and I will always try to do my best for you. But you must be aware that I know very little about modern, plastic dolls, and frankly, I care even less."

But like the lady in the Oscar Wilde play, who cared not a jot for music, but was extremely fond of musicians, I have always taken an obsessive interest in the vagaries of fashion, since I was quite a small boy. When I was seven years old, I made a paper doll of my clothes-horse sister, adding a dress almost every week. And in my time, I have been friends with some of the greatest designers, including Chanel and Schiaparelli, both of whom, I am proud to say, bought my paintings. So it was in an ambivalent state of mind that I read this book - and now my attitude to these dolls will never be the same.

It is written in Beau's inimitable style - and this I know, since I have sometimes tried to copy it - crisp, acerbic, all wit and brilliance, a joy to the eye as well as to the mind. But much more important to this reader, is the masterly way in which he sorts through the bewildering plethora of plastic fashion dolls, to arrive at their philosophical truth, and an almost Olympian judgment of their values.

An old dog can still learn new tricks. I can no longer maintain that superior, "I know better than you" attitude towards these modern, plastic mannequins - indeed, I shall now watch eagerly for each new fashion statement in miniature. You never know, I might even start collecting them!

John Darcy Noble
Curator of Toys, Emeritus, Museum of the City of New York

INTRODUCTION

By no means comprehensive, I have tried to limit the dolls featured in *Designer Fashion Dolls* to those actually bearing a designer endorsement, or to celebrity dolls which are attired in uncredited, albeit unmistakable designer duds. (Certain doll companies are so sensitive about their complicated licensing arrangements that they were prompted to question my first amendment rights during the writing of this promotional paean!) What celebrity doll (or, for that matter, celebrity) doesn't owe at least a part of their charisma to their dazzling designer subtext?

With the exception of the definitive Théatre de la Mode, and a few prototypical dolls, I also tried to limit the dolls to those available on a retail basis, in either the primary or secondary market, in the U.S.A. Wherever possible, I include current primary and secondary market prices for mint-in-box dolls and clothing. While at times I make passing reference to one-of-a-kind couture creations (usually made specifically for charitable occasions), prototypical designer dolls (which occur on an increasingly regular basis) are another volume altogether.

I excluded dolls and ensembles that (although attributed to famous designers) qualify as vintage costumes, as opposed to wearable 20th-Century attire. Many fanciful designs, however, qualify for what I refer to as "crossover costume;" as in something the *Gene®* doll might wear from a movie set to a cocktail party, (much as Elizabeth Taylor reportedly did during the filming of *Cleopatra*). As such, they reflect the costume quality of haute couture, and I included them.

In determining prices, I set them at the high end of the scale since I refer to that often mythic ideal, the "mint-in-box" doll. Much is made by marketing departments of "limited editions," and now "collector editions." All dolls, (even the ubiquitous *BARBIE®*), are produced in finite numbers; the smaller the company, the smaller the editions. Editions' limits are usually determined not only by the size of the company, but by the detailing of the doll, and its subsequent production cost. At Mattel, a limited edition means no more than 100,000 pieces world-

wide. (Their "collector editions" are more than 100,000 worldwide.) At Alexander, "limited edition" means no more than a couple thousand. Value inevitably fluctuates as collector consciousness evolves, and with the rise of the Internet, the doll market changes with cyber speed.

The word "couture" is tossed around like cotton candy on a stick in this guidebook. As such, the doll fashions featured in this tome that come close to couture (whose restrictions and rules are far too complicated for me to understand, much less clarify), would include Bradford Samuels' tiny recreations, along with the prototype Somers & Field dolls' one-of-a-kind, beautifully crafted attire. Ironically created for the doll least suited to wear clothing, Billy's one-of-a-kind Paul Smith outfit (made for a charity auction) also qualifies. BillyBoy's limited number of beautifully hand-crafted creations are certainly way beyond "bridgewear," the garment term for the bridge between ready-to-wear and haute couture. MACouture's exquisitely detailed dolls are equal, in the doll world, to shopping at the likes of Chanel and Prada in the "real" world. In my opinion, Madame Alexander's *Cissy*, *CoCo*, and *Jacqueline*, with their astonishing attire and accessories, are the most fashionable, rarefied and collectible designer fashion dolls currently on the mass-manufactured market. They reflect a new golden age of brilliant desirability at Alexander; their truly limited editions assuring their collectibility.

Designer fashion dolls define our dreams of uber style in miniature; all the better to handle the many irresistible options, from Christian Dior *BARBIE®* to Dior Ferre *BARBIE®* and back! In the immortal words of *Absolutely Fabulous'* Edina Monsoon, "Names, sweetie, names..."

THÉATRE DE LA MODE

Designed by Andre Beaurepaire, *Théatre de la Mode*'s "La Grotte Enchantee" includes fashions by Balenciaga and Madame Gres.

A collection comprised of 172, couture-clad, 27½-inch wire (with plaster head) mannequins, posing in a dozen stage settings designed by Europe's most brilliant artists and architects, the *Théatre de la Mode* was the brainchild of Robert Ricci, the son of fashion designer Nina Ricci. Opening at the Louvre in March, 1945, the exhibition featured exquisitely detailed, pragmatically miniature designs from France's leading couturiers, whose industry was in tatters from the ravages (and shortages) of World War II.

Intended to revive the post-war haute couture, as well as raise money for war relief, the ingenious exhibition captured the imagination of the European public. By 1946, the *Théatre* was captivating the United States on a tour that would end with its inclusion (with all but three of its original twelve settings) in the collection of the Maryhill Museum of Art in Goldendale, WA, where it has since been restored and had several revival tours. Beautifully captured in a wonderful Rizzoli / Metropolitan Museum of Art book, "The Theatre de la Mode" remains the definitive turning point in the evolution of the modern fashion doll.

Though purposefully designed not to look like dolls, the *Théatre de la Mode* mannequins nonetheless gave credence to a new generation that dolls didn't have to resemble children (which up until the early 1950's they usually did), but could actually fulfill the promise of adult sophistication, soon to be so brilliantly embodied by the all-powerful *BARBIE*®. Many doll designers featured in this book have credited the *Théatre de la Mode* for inspiration, including John Puzewski, BillyBoy, Mel Odom, and Bradford Samuels.

Rising from the ashes of war-ravaged France, the ingenious *THÉATRE DE LA MODE* is the prescient precursor of the modern designer fashion doll.

It seems *Cissy**, *CoCo**, and *Gene*®* (in her own tribute to Clair McCardle) have all resorted to taking summer stock of the Theatre de la Mode, here represented by a beachwear ensemble from Jacques Heim*.

Pioneers the first modern designer fashion dolls...

Ensembles from the French couture legend Elsa Schiaparelli, the elegantly edgy, surrealist-inspired, Italian-born fashion designer, were included in the *Théatre de la Mode*. Perhaps inspired by the success of that show, the by then venerable Schiaparelli made an agreement in 1951 with the American doll company Effanbee to create fashions for 14 special editions (in variations including walkers) of their popular 18-inch hard plastic *Honey*. Lavishly hyped and sumptuously attired, these special, limited-edition Sciaparelli *Honey* dolls were sold for upwards of $20.00 in the finest retail establishments (including Wanamaker's, Neiman-Marcus, Marshall-Field, and Abraham and Strauss). Billed as a "lady Honey" (instead of the more usual "girl Honey"), these decidedly adolescent dolls, due to their relative rarity, go for upwards of $800.00 (depending on style) in mint condition. Her pristine ball gown version can run into thousands of dollars.

EFFANBEE

In 1997, Effanbee recreated
an (uncredited) homage* to
this original Schiaparelli ball-
gowned beauty* from the
early 1950's.

*

SCHIAPARELLI VIRGA

*

Inspired by the success of Effanbee's beautiful interpretations , in 1956 Schiaparelli shrewdly created Schiaparelli Dolls, Ltd., in conjunction with a small doll company called Virga, which produced cheap and cheerful dress-up toddler dolls. The result was a sumptuously seductive, almost surrealistic line of hard-plastic, fully-jointed walker dolls, with vinyl heads and rooted hair. Marked "Virga" on the back of their beautifully realized heads, each fancifully profound outfit has the "handwritten" signature Schiaparelli label.

The line consists of three dolls, two roly-poly 8-inch toddler types aptly named *Tu Tu* (with green hair and matching ballet tutu, her toes en point), and usually pink-tressed *Go Go.** (*Go Go* was named after the designer's rather imperious daughter Yvonne, who was apparently even less amused at being a doll than at having that nickname.) Presented in visually arresting packaging featuring shiny black patent plastic contrasted with Schiaparelli's signature shocking pink, these dolls, with their presciently punk hair colors and rarefied, in-your-face frilliness, are most desirable.

A 12½-inch teen version, *Chi Chi,** had henna-red hair in an upsweep that the noted hairdresser Antoine had created for Schiaparelli in 1937. Her modest bustline and arched, high-heel-friendly feet had been introduced in America a year earlier by Madame Alexander. Chi Chi's extensive wardrobe, as those of her little compatriots, was of irresistible lavishness, supervised by

*

Schiaparelli with homages to all her classic innovations and touches, including curiously crafted milinary. A white tag tied with pink cord to *Chi Chi's* wrist reads: "created for you by Madame Elsa Schiaparelli, world-famous designer...your doll's clothes have been styled in Paris with the same skill lavished on expensive society gowns. Only the finest fabrics have been used. Additional clothing outfits* are available separately so you can build up your doll's personal wardrobe. Your Schiaparelli Doll comes to you in the jewel-like setting of her private studio box..."

Perhaps the most desirable *Chi Chi* is actually called "GoGo," in a special 1956 holiday edition put out by Bendel's. Sold in a plastic patent, pink and black box with several outfits, this 12½-inch teen "GoGo" (in fact *Chi Chi*) originally sold for $15.00, and would now go in mint-in-box condition for closer to $1,500.00. Most of the dressed, boxed Schiaparelli dolls were priced from $5.00 to $6.50 in the 1950's. Their beautifully-boxed fashions ranged from $3.00 to $5.00. Today, in mint condition, prices start at $150.00 and up for fashions, $500.00 and up for dolls.

While Madame Alexander set the standards for the first high-heeled, pre-*BARBIE*® fashion dolls of the 1950s, and the cosmetically promotional, and quite fashionable teenage *Coty, Toni,* and Revlon dolls were also very popular, Schiaparelli's Virga 12½-inch teenage doll is among the most desirable due to her delicious designer status. Effanbee's Schiaparelli *Honey,* presaging Alexander in her sumptuous suggestion of affluently sophisticated (albeit flat-chested and footed) adolescence, remains in a category all her prescient own.

MADAME ALEXANDER

In the early part of this century, from her kitchen table in some Siberian borough of NYC, self-proclaimed "Madame" Beatrice Alexander started what would become America's landmark upscale doll company. As innovative as she was savvy, Madame was among the first to license celebrity likenesses with the indomitable *Scarlett,* a doll she had the foresight to create upon reading *Gone With The Wind*, before the famous film version was made. In 1955, with the sophisticated, curvy spectre of Germany's *Bild Lily* doll engulfing the horizon, Madame was among the first to create a "teenage" American fashion doll. Named *Cissy*, this consummate clotheshorse had a semblance of a bustline (all the better to wear lingerie), and arched feet (all the better to wear high-heels).

While still juvenile in appearance (at least compared to *BARBIE®'s* forerunner *Lily*), *Cissy* was a definite evolution from the blatant babies so prevalent on the market. In Madame's own, wonderfully gender-free words, " There is no one who hasn't seen a child walking around in mother's high heels. A bra, too, and a dress or negligee can turn a hum-drum play day into a wonderful land of make-believe for a child...*Cissy*, the doll with the figure and features of a debutante, is the newest and most exciting doll in the world. Her long, slim body, her delicately molded bosom, her beautifully shaped feet that wear only high-heeled shoes made just for her and her elegant costumes designed for her alone, make *Cissy* the shining wonder of the doil world."

In the trend conscious toy world, fashion maven Madame must have noticed the success of Effanbee's sophisticated Schiaparelli *Honey*. As pragmatic as she was competitive, instead of licensing an expensive designer name she turned to her own ingenious design team, who already whipped up Madame's self-designed, personal wardrobe. The stunning, exquisitely realized results were a progression of fashion doll pizzazz that had already netted Madame and her staff four successive Fashion Academy Gold Medal Awards, (the equivalent of today's prestigious Council of Fashion Designers/CFDA Award), in 1951-54.

CISSY & MA COUTURE

The exquisite, late 1950s, vintage 21-inch *Cissy**, courtesy of Mel Odom, is hard plastic with jointed vinyl arms and jointed knees. Her glued-on, honey blonde wig also came in brown, or red. She has hazel-colored sleep eyes. *Cissy* came in both walking and non-walking versions, and sold, depending on attire, for around $25.00 in better department stores. Today, in mint-condition, she goes for $500.00 and up.

The first reissue edition, '96 *Cissy,* also 21-inch, is hard vinyl with soft vinyl head and arms. Still jointed at the knees from her original two-piece hard-plastic mold, her arm joints have been retired and she no longer walks. *Cissy's* sleep eyes are now deepest brown and her glued-on acrylic wig is a ravishing red. Her rare and astounding African-American version*, with black hair, has one of the most striking countenances ever created. Most dramatic are *Cissy's* newly created coiffures and maquillage, the work of beauty maven Mathu Anderson, who, along with designer Puzewski, is well-established among fashion's cutting edge. Primarily priced in the $350.00 to $750.00 range, opulantly attired and accessorized *Cissy* is no cheap date.

17

Circa 1958, a series of *Cissy*'s help Madame ascend to the heights of doll fashion.

JOHN PUZEWSKI

By the mid-1960s, hard-plastic, 21-inch *Cissy* fell out of fashion; her brilliant couture profile obscured by vinyl, 11½-inch *BARBIE®'s* much more accessible, affordable shadow. Decades passed, and in 1990, well past 90, so did Madame. Her company, sold several times, hired a fashion wunderkind named John Puzewski in 1994. Several regimes later, he continues to give the Alexander Doll Company the most prestigious profile on the fashion doll runway. Directing a brilliant team of designers, Puzewski 's intuitive resurrection of *Cissy* and his creation of MACOUTURE has no doubt kept Beatrice happily beaming downward, no small feat in itself!

John Puzewski spoke with me on behalf of the *Doll Journal* in 1997: "I chose fashion as a career at an early age, considering it only from the highest standards, interning at Herrera, Halston, and Scaasi — places with a similar taste level to my own, where you created beauty, not T-shirts. By the time I got to Byron Lars, the taste level overall in the fashion world was diminishing. After he had to close, I realized I was faced with either a fake fur mentality or a move to Paris. I am a New Yorker, so I opted for dolls. Madame Alexander was the perfect venue..."

"Seeing the original *Cissy* made me want to give her a dramatic comeback. I added jointing, elongated her neck, gave her larger breasts; her arms are thinner and she now swivels at the waist...it is essential to articulate movement to capture her style completely... The whole object of doing *Cissy* was to bring fashion to people who normally wouldn't wear couture but love to live the fantasy of it. I gave *Cissy* her own unique taste that she will always keep, so that each season she can choose new looks and the collector can live through her. People are used to dolls in ball gowns, which of course you have to offer, but the fact that she has a suit and a crocodile handbag similar to something they have just seen in a fashion magazine is very appealing..."

"I loved the similar-sized dolls from the 40's French *Théatre de la Mode*. The detail they could get in shoes and bags...once you get past a certain size you really lose the details...Halston worked in half-scale. When I used to work at

Original sketch by John Puzewski.

Halston, they would always have these half-scale dresses. He would take them out to his beach house and drape, and then he would bring them back on the half-scale. They'd make the corrections and get it back to full scale, so there were quite a few of these half-scale dress editions..."

"Madame Alexander (MA) Couture was a whole new concept. I had to make it like actual clothing you would wear, with a bit of fantasy and built-in nostalgia. As far as mixing prints and colors as fashion is today, that took some grasping...you could tell them (the toy executives) chartreuse is the big color this year and they would just look at you and suggest their all time favorite color...When I put two different zebra prints together, I had to pull out fashion magazines to finally prove it was acceptable...I'm trying to take the collector to a different plane...You do that gradually with the customer, so that they understand what you are doing...Eventually, you can take them to the very top of fantasy!"

Cissy Ebony & Ivory Houndstooth Suit.

Bloomingdale's Coral &
Leopard *Cisette*.

Cissy Coral & Leopard
Travel ensemble.

22

Cissy Venice.

Cissy Onyx, Velvet
& Lace.

Cissy Cafe Rose and Ivory cocktail dress.

Cissy Barcelona.

Cissy Milan.

Cissy Paris.

Coco

With the success of *Cissy's* 1996 revival, the next year Alexander reintroduced their gorgeously revamped, 16-inch vinyl *CoCo*. Billed as *Cissy's* younger cousin, this prettiest in pink blonde is spectacular enough to ravishingly reinstate that all too often tired combination. Sold dressed in her "*CoCo* and Cleo Travel Abroad"* suit ensemble (including her Maltese Cleo*) for approximately $300.00 ,

Coco's irresistible "Capri Sightseeing" and "Cocktail Enchantment"* ensembles and accessories are sold separately, each for approximately $100.00. The doll can also be purchased with all these ensembles for approximately $400.00. For 1998, there is *CoCo* "Belle Epoch"*, which comes with two dramatic ensembles and one doll for approximately $300.00. Due to her incredible pizzazz, *Coco's* collectibility seems assured.

*

*

Alexander's Liberace serenades *Cissy*, resplendent in her Calla Lily evening column and bolero.

CHARLOTTE JOHNSON

The Designer Of *BARBIE®'s* First Fashion Epochs, Deftly Defines 20th Century French Couture, In Miniature, For The Masses…

If ever there was a relationship destined in retail heaven, it was that between Mattel's dynamic co-founder (and *Barbie's* "mother") Ruth Handler, and Charlotte Johnson, the detail-obsessed designer responsible for creating *Barbie's* premiere fashion collection. A sublimely sophisticated, single, 40-something veteran (since the age of 17) of New York's Seventh Avenue, "career girl" Johnson had relocated to Los Angeles, where she moonlighted as a teacher at the Chouinard Art School, while working as a dress designer in the Los Angeles garment industry. The school recommended Charlotte when Ruth's husband and partner, Elliot, inquired about someone who could design a line of doll clothing for mass production, in preparation for Ruth's revolutionary fashion doll project, *Barbie.*

In her autobiography, *Dream Doll*, Ruth Handler says that the diligent Johnson, initially keeping both of her jobs, "worked out of her apartment at night making the first Barbie clothes. I'd go there two or three nights a week to work out the line with her. We developed about twenty outfits, some of them very glamorous numbers…" Disagreeing with both the designer and Mattel's advertising agency, Handler insisted teenagers would relate to more mundane ensembles, however "I began to lose the battle because consumers seemed to prefer the glamorous side of Barbie."

Soon working full-time at Mattel, Johnson couldn't find small-scale fabrics and prints appropriate for doll-sized fashions. The sheer volume required meant that Mattel would have to create their own fabrics, which could best be accomplished in Japan. Before she could say "sayonara," Johnson found herself elegantly ensconced in Tokyo's Imperial Hotel, where she and several other Mattel employees spent three years establishing Mattel's Japanese manufacturing operations. Perfectionist Johnson worked six days a week with a Japanese designer and two seamstresses, devising minimally sewn designs stressing proportion. Her keen grasp of scale assured the fit of each costume approximated that on a real fashion model. To accomodate this, BARBIE® doll was designed with unrealistic anatomical proportions which help create a realistic look when modelling her fashions. Charlotte's legendary "fussiness" led to the obtaining of crucial, small-scaled

career girl   *junior designer*   *fashion editor*

fabrics and prints, along with tiny snaps, buttons, and zippers. As Johnson supervised, exquisitely realized little garments were being pristinely delegated from factory to housewives, who added fine finishing touches, while other home workers sewed the ensembles into their packaging cards.

The image for *BARBIE*® (named after the Handler's teenage daughter, Barbara, who forbid her mother to refer to her as BARBIE® thereafter) was said to be based much more on Charlotte Johnson's own statuesque, 5' 10-inches (in heels) silhouette. Ruth's late son, Ken Handler, insisted (to his mother's denials) that both Charlotte's hair and maquillage were complete-ly like the doll when he first met her in the early 1960s. Certainly, in 1959 as an eight-year-old, my image of this original, soignée BARBIE® was that of a woman closer to my impossibly chic mother's (then 30ish) age, than that of an 18 year-old.

CJ, as she became known to her staff, went to the Paris couture collections seasonally, borrowing the best from the likes of Dior, St. Laurent, Givency, and Balenciaga. Her designs were American reflections of French fashion, right down to naming each ensemble in the manner of the haute couture at that time. Her rav-ishing reinterpretations of real couture, mass manufactured right down to their sumptuous silk linings, made a lasting impression of

Busy Gal
BARBIE®

impeccable taste on a huge number of baby boomers, who were exposed regu-larly to them. Unlike the upscale Alexanders, *BARBIE*® was sold at Sears (and everywhere else), for $3.00. Her fashions ranged from $1.50 up to $10.00 for spe-cial gift sets. Now a #1 *BARBIE*®, in mint-condition, goes for $5,000.00 and up. Her 1960's wardrobe, mint, can be in the hundreds of dollars; with rare examples from the collection, including "Gay Parisienne," going for over a thousand dollars. Fitting monetary tributes to their Alzheimers-stricken designer who, more than any other, brought the most sophisticated designer taste to the impressionable masses.

33

GAY PARISIENNE

The most sophisticated, sought after, and rare of BARBIE®'s original, 1959 fashion collection is "Gay Parisienne." Described by BARBIE® fashion historian Sara Sink Eames, in her thorough Collector Books' masterpiece *Barbie Fashions, Vol I*, as "the ultimate in late 50's glamour — the bubble dress! This ensemble is definitely one of the most desirable, not only for its rarity but for its beauty and significance in depicting the high style of the period." Though appearing briefly and almost mythologically in only the first collection, (and known by children more from its depiction on BARBIE®*'s* box,* long after the dress was discontinued), "Gay Parisienne" (including white rabbit fur stole, veiled headband, long white tricot gloves, gold velvet clutch, deep blue open toe pumps, and graduated pearl necklace and earrings) made a strong enough impression on style conscious baby boomers to be revived in 1991 as the first release in the Porcelain Treasures Collection* of 11½-inch BARBIE® dolls from Mattel. Originally deep blue pindot rayon taffeta, this terrific reproduction's dress is now deep blue pindot microfiber,* underneath which is a light blue repro lingerie set with an update of garters and seamed stockings. Originally around $200.00, this doll has now doubled in price and remains popular with many collectors usually put off by porcelain.

Other delectible homages to "Gay Parisienne" include Hallmark's two-dimensional greeting card,* and Peck-Aubrey's paper doll rendition.*

 *

 *

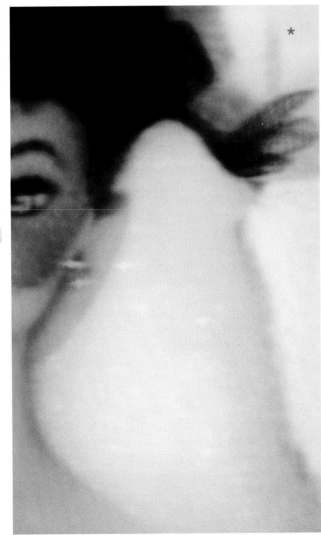 *

 *

Just as omnipresent BARBIE®'s
sublimely sophisticated wardrobe
reflected fancy French fashion, so the
obscure *Miss Seventeen's* astonishing attire is all-
American...

      Spawned by the phenomenal success of the early BARBIE® doll, Louis Marx & Co., Inc.'s *Miss Seventeen*, which debuted in 1961, can trace her roots to BARBIE®'s predecessor, the decidedly downscale (albeit irresistible) German *Bild Lily* doll, from whose mold *Miss Seventeen* was cast. Several things distinguish *Miss Seventeen* from the dubious digression of *Lily*/BARBIE® duplicates that inevitably flooded the market once BARBIE® began making retail history. Notorious for cheaply knocking off trendy toys, Marx countered its pragmatic methods with visual appeal that has, in retrospect, made their toys much beloved and valued collectibles. In the case of *Miss Seventeen*, Marx cleverly commissioned the design team of Jay E. Watkins and Edward Roberts, founders of New York City's famed Fashion Institute of Technology, to create a dazzlingly designed and packaged wardrobe of a dozen distinctly American-inspired fashions.

      Though herself poorly executed, *Miss Seventeen* is ravishingly redeemed by her brilliantly conceived wardrobe. Made, like most *Lily* hybrids, in Hong Kong, *Miss Seventeen* came in both 15-inch and 18-inch hard plastic versions. It was clearly her incredible clothing that was the hook in distracting consumers from 11½-inch BARBIE®. If you wanted the wonderful wardrobe, you had to buy the doll to model it. Lavishly illustrated in a fold-out fashion poster, each ensemble came in a dramatically packaged black "fashion book," with a front window pocket containing the outfit,* opening to a sketch of the fashion and chicly titled description,* along with the legend "CREATED ESPECIALLY FOR MISS SEVENTEEN BY THE FASHION INSTITUTE OF TECHNOLOGY BY JAY

E. WATKINS & EDWARD ROBERTS." A stark black box with "Miss Seventeen...A Beauty Queen" written across it in sophisticated script contained the doll, which came dressed in a black one-piece bathing suit, white satin-lined red cape, yellow ribbon-trimmed white banner with the "Miss Seventeen" signature, red heels, and beautifully molded gold plastic crown and inscribed gold plastic pageant trophy.

Unlike her playfully prurient predecessor *Lily*, *Miss Seventeen* appeared to be as hard as her "Jungle Red" nails. Her more mature, dominatrix demeanor featured flaring, red-painted nostrils and white painted pupils, gave her an aggressively unsettling edge. This aside, several factors doomed *Miss Seventeen* to rarefication. The future for fashion dolls was about bendable and glowing, not about brittle and laminated. Her larger size also worked against her.

Truly representative of her atomic times, *Miss Seventeen* was also doomed to literally self-destruct. Fragile to begin with, it is not easy to find her in mint-condition. She is often chipped, particularly her fingers. Though beautifully constructed, her clothing tends to fall to pieces. This may be due to a chemical reaction, since with some dolls the bathing suit has to be peeled off and often disintegrates. *Miss Seventeen* has also been known to go to pieces, as she is strung together with elastic cord that has a tendency to dry rot. Her unrooted hair, which comes in a pony-tail style and a harder-to-find, elaborately upswept bun, is a wig. Glued onto her head, it can become extremely messy. (A signature *Lily* spit curl is only suggested on my own *Miss Seventeen* by an odd bump on her forehead, which is one of many discolored glue marks on the messily manufactured doll.) Her hair comes in brown, black, "brownette", and an extremely rare (if not legendary) red.

While *Lily* now goes for upwards of a thousand dollars, *Miss Seventeen* can still be had for about $350.00. As disarming as she is alarming, her relative rarity, currently fashionable size, and perverse pedigree (involving a patent lawsuit with Mattel, eventually thrown out of court by an exasperated judge) make *Miss Seventeen* deliciously desirable to collectors. Her extremely rare wardrobe, with its emphasis on American style (as opposed to BARBIE®'s French couture leanings) is particularly precious. It is also relatively inexpensive, going mint-in-portfolio box for about $250.00. As illustrated in her poster, these fashions are the perfect compliment to *Miss Seventeen's* intensely vivid image as the fiercely independent American woman, striving for "the best of everything".

*

A FASHION FAVORITE for . . .

Miss Seventeen...

"RAGE OF PARIS"

A lovely lady just passed by! It's Miss Seventeen in her very first Paris creation. Just wait 'til you see your teenage miss turn into a glamorous lady of fashion the moment she puts on this beautiful gown. Now add the perfect finishing touch — a hat and a muff of scarlet velvet that just match the rose at her waist! Don't you think she should have hosts of admirers to whisper sweet nothings in her pretty ear?

MISS SEVENTEEN'S "RAGE OF PARIS"

FASHION BOOK CONTAINS:

- Black Gown With Red Rose
- Velvet Hat
- Velvet Muff
- Panties
- Petticoat
- Pearls
- Umbrella
- Black Sandals

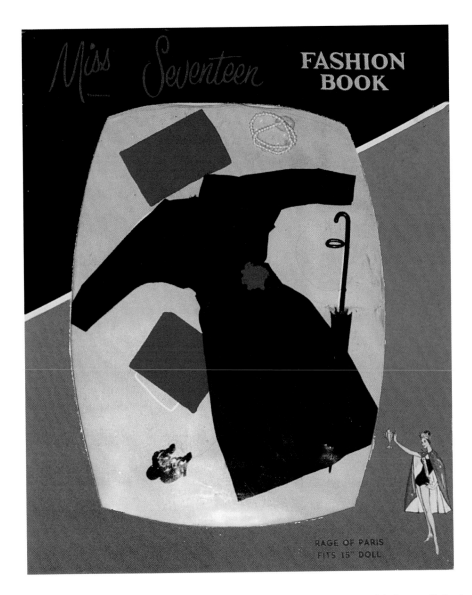

Despite its fancy French name, *Miss Seventeen's* Rage of Paris ensemble has a distinctly American flair. The sophisticated black "faille" dress features incredible detail, including an intricately paneled skirt with separate black net petticoat.

IT'S A MOD MOD MOD MOD WORLD

*

Marx Braniff/Pucci Air Hostesses

Best known for their colorful molded plastic and tin lithograph playsets and doll houses, in 1967 Marx manufactured Braniff Airlines' Emilio Pucci designed uniforms, in an 11½-inch fashion doll size. Pucci was incredibly hot at this time, worn often by the ubiquitous celebrity likes of "Valley of the Dolls" author Jacqueline Susann. His designs for the Texas-based airlines Braniff, which also featured brightly colored airplanes, garnered much attention.

Hawking the Emilio Pucci/Braniff designer hook, Montgomery Ward sold gift sets of four ensembles, including blue knit "Hostess Pajamas;" a beautifully constructed, A-line broadcloth "Pucino Serving Dress" in rose and pale yellow; an outrageous lime green and yellow twill coat "Boarding Outfit;" and a two-piece, chain accessorized "Rasberry Suit." These came with a fully-jointed vinyl fashion doll. The outfits were also sold separately as "pac" ensembles by Mattel, who licensed the designs from Marx. There were also two different sets of lingerie, and a pilot outfit that came on a Mattel standard #750 *Ken* doll. Often mistaken as Mattel Japanese manufactured designs, in fact these tantalizing treasures were manufactured by Marx, in Hong Kong, with great details; including magnificently molded shoes and boots, Pucci print scarves tied over pill box hats, oversize zippers, knit gloves, and a clear, round plastic helmet!

Each ensemble came with a Braniff luggage tag on a gold chain, along with a photograph of the outfit on a live model. Originally selling for about $10.00, the four ensembles, mint-in-box with a *Lily*-type "bubble cut" fashion doll, now go for upwards of $2,000.00. Selling initially for about $3.00 each, the Mattel-licensed Braniff "pac" ensembles go for upwards of $350.00 each, mint on card. Originally about $5.00, a pristine Braniff *Ken* now goes for upwards of $500.00. Just as *Miss Seventeen's* stylish silhouette personified the Camelot consciousness of the early 60s, six years later these marvelous uniforms are quintessentially "mod."

40

THE ONGOING BRITISH INVASION:
TWIGGY

As the 60s progressed, and Camelot came to an abrupt halt, the Beatles bounced over from formerly dreary, suddenly swinging Britain. This Mod "British Invasion" permeated the U.S. with a playful sense of POP, which has been reinventing itself ever since. From Mary Quant to Princess Diana, the Great in Britain means fashion. Dolls based on British fashion celebrities have flourished in the U.S. since 1967, with the introduction of one that remains the most collectible of the lot — Mattel's *Twiggy*.

*

42

HERE SHE IS!

TWIGGY GEAR #1728 $2.75 TWIGSTER #1727 $2.75 TWIGGY-DO'S #1725 $2.75 TWIGGY TURNOUTS #1726 $2.75

©1967 Minnow Co., Ltd. and Twiggy Enterprises, Ltd.

More than any other supermodel, (a term she was the first to personify), Cockney-born, 17 year old Twiggy (aka Lesley Hornby) caught the imagination of mid-1960's teenagers (and the attention of their perplexed parents) around the world. One of the first fashion models to cross over into the consciousness of the general public, (due as much to curiosity as appreciation), Twiggy was completely innocent — and "Totally Now!" Like Audrey Hepburn, Twiggy was a fashion illustration come-to-life*. Her waif-like image was marketed on everything from false eyelashes to panty-hose.* Nobody could resist her, and from her myriad, vivid visual impressions in the likes of Diana Vreeland's *Vogue*, Twiggy's early image remains a refreshing, reusable fashion icon.

This British mass-market marvel was not lost on Mattel, who, faced with reflecting political havoc on the home front, was quick to come up with an 11-1/2-inch *Twiggy* doll,* one of BARBIE®*'s* "trendy" British "friends". The doll was the same mold, with different coiffure and maquillage, as BARBIE®*'s* "British cousin" *Casey*. She had a much smaller, rounder bustline than her curvier American cousin, to accommodate the mod silhouette that had a few years previously revolutionized world fashion.

Thanks to Mary Quant's "invention" of panty hose in the early 1960s, women (along with their "reflection" BARBIE®) were no longer (at least, unwillingly) confined in panties, girdles, garters, and stockings. The emphasis had shifted from curvy, career-girl to epicene teen. Still under Charlotte Johnson's fashion supervision, Mattel adjusted brilliantly. Their *Twiggy* doll came dressed in four brightly mod ensembles that could be purchased separately.* They were called "Twiggy Gear," "Twigster," "Twiggy Do's," and "Twiggy Turnouts," and sold for $2.75. Today Mattel's *Twiggy* doll, mint-in-box, is in the $1,200.00 range; her mint-in-box costumes are upwards of $250.00.

Twiggy, now in mid-life and also known as Lesley Lawson, is one of the few people with a doll namesake who doesn't seem to resent it. In addition to consistently acting on the stage, in films and television both here and in England, she has even done an infomercial on BARBIE® Collectibles for her former licenser Mattel.

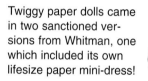

Twiggy paper dolls came in two sanctioned versions from Whitman, one which included its own lifesize paper mini-dress!

44

Unofficial *Wiggy* paper dolls,
from Artcraft, came with a wardrobe of
card board doll wigs.

MARY QUANT

Legendary British designer Mary Quant personified the Mod mentality; in everything from fashions and cosmetics to the panty hose she created to enable women to wear her fashions in the first place. Her ingenious marketing of the mini-skirt helped catapult the revolutionary British mod movement to the forefront of 1960's international design. In the early 1970s, Gabriel Industries of Hagerstown, Maryland, released in the United States a delightful 9-inch vinyl doll, made by Model Toys Ltd. of Shotts, Lanarkshire, Scotland. Named *Daisy,*

after Mary Quant's famous "flower power" logo, the doll came colorfully window-packaged in a quintessentially 70's orange, ochre, pink, scarlet, and black box. Dressed in a variety of incredibly chic ensembles, she was qualified as a genuine designer doll by a pink daisy corner logo stating "Fashions for Daisy by Mary Quant". Her extended side-flap proclaims "the only doll with real-life fashions by Mary Quant."

At least 16 different ensembles came arrestingly packaged with the legend "More stunning fashions for Daisy by Mary Quant / Internationally famous designer Mary Quant makes Daisy the best-dressed doll in the world." Though her fashions reflect real Quant designs from the 1970s, a decade as generally cheesy as the previous had been profound, their simplified doll proportions are evocative of the more stunningly straightforward 1960s.

Beautifully made in Hong Kong, the nine fashions are engagingly presented as fashion sketches on the back of the boxes.* Another creation, a beautiful black satin pantsuit not represented on either box I have, is called "Posh."* I purchased it during its original retail run at Bloomingdale's, for the sticker price of $2.25. The doll, as I recall, was less than $10.00 at that time. Today, somewhat obscure, Mary Quant's *Daisy,* mint-in-box, goes for around $150.00, her mint-in-box costumes for $75.00 and up. The real Mary Quant still runs a huge fashion empire from London, and is worth considerably more!

Gene® fashion designers Doug James and Laura Meisner (the latter's two *Gene®* creations, "Iced Coffee" and "Embassy Luncheon" are great favorites among collectors) have come up with their own prototype dolls, vibrantly representing two 16-year-old British girls whose fathers own a mythical mod department store called "Somers & Field" Somewhat *Cissy*-fied, these two nubile 17-inch vinyl dolls, who are strung with elastic as opposed to socket jointing, are named *Daisy Field* and *Willow Somers.* Also evocative of teenage *Absolutely Fabulous' Patsy* and *Edina*, they model fashions as amazingly detailed as their initial concept. Hopefully, they will be commercially realized; seeming so ripe for a retro-visionary company like Effanbee to develop into a prestige "bridge" line.

VIVIENNE WESTWOOD

One of this century's most forward fashion designers, Vivienne Westwood is in a class all her own due to her ingenious ability to, through her innovative interpretations, brilliantly illuminate the most obscure fashion movements and expose them as major trends. Assigned by *Interview* magazine ten years ago to write up the already legendary designer and expecting a safety-pinned punk nightmare, I was delighted to find Westwood as down to earth as she was over-the-top.

Clad in faded jeans, work boots, a Ralph Lauren cardigan "I bought on sale last year," and no make-up, Westwood told me she was born into the working class in the quaintly rural Northern English town of Tintwhistle. "Living there gave me a lot of confidence...people born in a big town like London do have a sense that the world's a restricted place..."

Westwood, who told me her favorite pastime was staying in bed with a good book, was certainly prescient on the current ubiquity of twin sets when she told me, "The Queen wears really lovely knitwear...I love twin sets and pearls...let me tell you about who my favorite designer is, talking about the Queen. Really I think that Norman Hartnell, who used to design the Queen's dresses, is fabulous. The Queen's coronation dress is one of the best things that was ever done because it made her look so important."

About the already ubiquitous Princess Diana, Westwood said candidly, and again preciently, "To be honest, I haven't met her, because she didn't speak to me. I was in a room with some other fashion designers, and there must have been one or two people who she didn't notice, and I was one of them...I love the way she dresses...this is not to take the piss out of her, but my attraction to these things is it's BARBIE® doll clothes. The whole matching thing that is really, really nice...she's got quite nice posture, doesn't she, and a nice figure...she looks thinner and thinner all the time...I don't like her hairstyle though, it's just all that mess in the front. Can you imagine if she just took her hair and parted it like a little girl's?"

The September, 1998 issue of *Barbie Bazaar* offered a limited edition (of only 1,000) Vivienne Westwood Life Ball BARBIE®s,* made in association with Austrian AIDS Organizations, at a retail cost of $500.00 each. With hairstyle realized by the Austrian Grecht Company, thigh-length earrings from French jewelry designer Laurent Rivaud, (and validated by Westwood's own logo in metal), this astounding, relatively rare reflection of Westwood's profound style is one of the most important dolls (and best investments) featured in this tome.

Life Ball
Barbie

*

PRINCESS DIANA

An uneven plethora of dolls (in every conceivable material) pay tribute to Britain's tragic Princess Diana. I am dumfounded at the sheer scope! As such, I have chosen to present but five; two in porceline, and three in vinyl. Though these dolls qualify as celebrity character (as opposed to celebrity designer) dolls, all but two feature uncredited gowns created by the more mature Diana's brilliant "state occasion" designer, Catherine Walker.*

With fabrics and detailing on each gown fit for a real princess, kitschmeister Franklin Mint's two 17½-inch "porceline portrait dolls," titled *Diana, Princess of Wales** and *Diana, Princess of Style** are currently advertised on the primary market for the famous five payments of $39.00 respectively. Their more awkward, 15-inch vinyl version titled *Diana, The People's Princess,** features a separately sold wardrobe fit for a Sloane Ranger. The doll, dressed in an off-the-rack representation of a Chanel (referrered to as "a stylish light blue suit") is $90.00, each separate outfit approximately $45.00.

*

GATCO's 16-inch vinyl *Diana, Princess of Wales,** is beautifully dressed and accessorized in a glittering, graceful gown (uncredited) by Catherine Walker. She is currently on the primary market for $125.00. Alexander's 10-inch *People's Princess** is wearing an uncredited representation of what is described, in Tim Graham and Tamsin Blanchard's Welcome Rain book *Dressing Diana**, as "an elaborate piece of haute couture by Victor Edelstein." The doll retails for approximately $125.00. As the best of the current lot, these Diana dolls are sure to accrue in value, particularly if the late Princess's saga continues to unfold in such a fascinating manner. At the time of publication, the Franklin Mint was reported by the *New York Post* to be in "embarrassing" legal wrangles with The Princess Diana Foundation, which might also affect collectibility.

Diana...

Evolution of a
Princess

53

SINDY
AND THE
EMANUEL'S

Hasbro's 11½-inch British fashion doll *Sindy*, available here on the secondary market, had four spectacular gowns designed for her in 1985 by the British designers David and Elizabeth Emanuel, famous for making Princess Diana's wedding gown. Titled "High Society," "Romantica," "Scarlet Lady,"* and "Misty Mauve," (in, respectively, pink, yellow, red and black, and mauve and black), these exquisitely detailed ball gowns came window-boxed with the legend: "Designer Fashion: The Emanuel Collection."

"Four *Sindy* fashions, exclusively created by these famous designers whose clients include celebrities and Royalty. Full of detail and style, complete with accessories, these fashions are rightly at the top of *Sindy*'s 1985 fashion collection."

They are also at the top of any designer fashion doll collector's list. Highly desirable, and difficult to find, these mint-in-box fashions, which originally sold at Harrod's for the British equivalent of approximately $15.00, today go for upwards of $150.00.

With the smashing success of their first signature *Sindy* line, the Emanuels designed another line for 1986. This consisted of a pleated, shin-length, sailor-style navy and white pinstripe day dress with white sailor collar trimmed in navy ribbon, leg-o-mutton, white-cuffed sleeves, matching hat, and a shoulder strap umbrella. Originally about $10.00 in U.S. money, this mint-in-box outfit is, today, around $75.00.

A gorgeous black, strapless ball gown with a shaped bodice and full over-skirt of black and gold lurex net is tied just below the knee with a big fuchsia bow. Of special interest to those who collect specifically black-colored designer doll clothing, this gown, which also sold originally at Harrod's for approximately $15.00, now goes, mint-in-box, for upwards of $175.00.

*

The crowning glory of this collection was a luxurious lingerie ensemble which is described by *Sindy* historian Colette Mansell in her colorful and comprehensive volume, *The History of Sindy*, as " probably the most glamorous set ever to be produced for a doll." Made of cream silk and trimmed with white lace, it included a bra, "French knickers", a garter belt, cream stockings, and a camisole that could be worn under a matching, floor-length negligee. Also originally sold for approximately $15.00 at Harrod's, it is now, mint-in-box, worth about $175.00.

54

HASBRO'S MODELS

*

Recently discontinued on the primary market, *Sindy's* last reflection of designer status came with the release on the European market of her three "supermodel friends," *Claudia Schiffer, Naomi Campbell,** and *Karen Muldar.* Released in 1995 by Hasbro International, these three 11½-inch, vinyl dolls came in colorful, multilingual packaging. Each says the model "…has participated in the creation of the outfit worn by the doll." (Ms. Schiffer certainly came up with a saucily revealing stunner!) Made with Hasbro's high quality, these dolls became instantly desirable to both collectors of fashion and celebrity dolls. Though new, they were sold here initially on the secondary market for about $45.00 (as opposed to their European price of approximately $25.00), and are sure to accrue in value due in part to the fact that, in 1997, *Sindy's* being sold down the river Thames (so to speak) relegated her to the status of a secondary market marvel.

*

MATCHBOX'S MODELS

In 1989, the U.S. division of Britain's Matchbox Toys released 11½-inch, vinyl doll representations of American supermodels Christie Brinkley, Beverly Johnson, and Cheryl Tiegs. Individually boxed as "The Real Model Collection — The Most Beautiful Models In The World!", each doll "Comes with Change-Around Fashion Portfolio, Beauty Secrets Booklet and Autographed Photo!" While my Beverly Johnson more resembles a fanciful "Malibu Julia Louise-Dreyfus," just so you aren't confused, on the back of her box is a "clip 'n save" color photo and "resume", along with glossy photos of all three models with their dolls, under the positive legend "We're all friends in The Real Model Collection." Each sold for $14.99 at the most lamented Lionel Kiddy City, and can still be picked up on the secondary market for a relative song (about $35.00, mint-in-box) today.

Christie Brinkley   Beverly Johnson   Cheryl Tiegs

55

GIRLS™

The latest British invasion is embodied by the scintillating, and (in the context of pop) appropriately short-lived, Spice Girls.* Fast-forward, San Francisco-based toy company Galoob was quick to come up with two sets of vibrantly realized, 11½-inch, vinyl Spice Girls* dolls; edition two representing the Spice Girls "On Tour."* Wearing dazzling designs based on their actual performance wardrobes (culled from the best of British boutique fashion), The Spice Girls dolls made their debut at the 1998 Toy Fair.

Quickly appearing both here and in Britain, the dolls just as quickly became unavailable. By the time the "On Tour" dolls arrived, *Ginger Spice** had already left the group, and these dolls also vanished in a collector frenzy. Due to Galoob's practice of unevenly shipping the individual dolls (i.e. skimping on *Scary Spice*,* in an outmoded marketing practice), complete sets of Spice Girls became even more difficult to obtain. Almost immediately upon their respective debuts, both sets of five dolls (which sold individually at K-Mart for $12.99) began to be sold on the secondary market, as complete sets only, for up to $150.00. Recently, while K-Mart offered nonexistent Spice Girl On Tour dolls for $9.99, the local Toys R Us served up dozens of the tour dolls (sans *Ginger*), proving that (for me at least) all Scary things come to those who wait.

Two Spice Girls playsets were also shown at Toy Fair; a "Superstar Dressing Room"* and a "Spice Sound Stage."* The catalog states, with a sticker, that the dressing room had already been "dropped" from production, while the sound stage, if produced, has the status of hen's teeth. Subjectively speaking, both could be considered priceless.

HOLLYWOOD:

Beyond the valley of designer dolls...

OLEG CASSINI

Hollywood fashion at its illusory best is classic, simply-stated, unadulterated glamour. Perhaps the best example of this is a timeless dress worn by legendary film star Gene Tierney, in the 1940's cinema version of Somerset Maugham's *The Razors Edge*. Meant to seduce Tyrone Power on a whirlwind night out in Paris, the black, floor-length fringe dress, with black fringe shawl, set the mood for one of the most memorable staircase descents* in cinema history. The designer of that dress, (and the husband of the star who wore it), was Oleg Cassini.

"It has lived through the times, that dress," Mr. Cassini told me in an interview related to this book, "I had no control of this, though I include a fringe dress in most of my collections since, in tribute..." Now, almost half a century later, Mr.Cassini has endorsed his first doll, in tribute to another legend close to his heart, Jackie Kennedy.

Born a count in Czarist Russia, fashion luminary Oleg Cassini was raised in Italy. Finding fame as a costume designer in Hollywood, he became one of its most glamorous denizens. Married for a time to movie star Gene Tierney, he was later engaged to pre-princess Grace Kelly. The prototypical jet-setter, Mr. Cassini managed to maintain his position as a member of European society, beginning his own New York City-based fashion empire in the 1950s.

In 1960, Mr. Cassini's reputation was certified in pure gold when he was chosen by new First Lady Jackie Kennedy, then assuredly conceptualizing the legendary Camelot look, to be her official White House fashion designer. The seamless Cassini combination of European sophistication and uniquely Hollywood-American savvy helped place the brilliant Jackie permanently at the forefront of international fashion and celebrity.

Following 1997's lavishly-illustrated Rizzoli publication of his Jackie memoirs, *A Thousand Days of Magic*, Cassini has endorsed a 15½-inch vinyl doll from The Franklin Mint. Trademarked as *The Jackie Doll*,* she is "The first heirloom doll authentically dressed in a stunning fashion by Oleg Cassini, creator of the legendary 'Jackie Look.' " With status-quo suave, Cassini told me that "I acquainted myself early on with toy soldiers," and also a favorite childhood set of Lenci cowboys and Indians. "I always had a feeling for dolls, but it was dormant until this *Jackie*."

Though many different "Jackies" have been made over the years, this is the first one "officially" approved by anyone near her, due to the fact that, in a lifetime of noblesse oblige, Jackie would never endorse the commercialization of her likeness. "Jackie was a very private person," said Cassini pragmatically, "When the (estate) sale occurred, the mood changed..."

Five Cassini classics, including three day dresses representing official visits to Paris, India, and Ottowa, as well as a pink ruffled gown worn on her triumphant trip to Paris, and Jackie's spectacular white satin gown worn "on her historic state visit to India" (which comes dressed on the doll) are included in the collection, along with the inevitable trunk.* The doll, as uncanny as a vinyl likeness of Jackie can be, is available for "five monthly installments of $18.00 each." Her fashions, each "only one installment of $45.00," come accessorized with (among other things) the obligatory pill box hat, head-scarf, and prescient Onassis sunglasses!* Another famous Cassini design can be found on a somewhat earlier edition, 16¼-inch Franklin Mint "Inaugural Ball Porcelain Portrait Doll"* of Jackie, wearing Cassini's (uncredited) classic white Inauguration gown, selling on the primary market for approximately $200.00. Jackie represented the apotheosis of attainment during her lifetime, as she seemingly remains for retail eternity.

In 1964, a doll was produced by Ross Products, Inc., and named for the 17-year-old daughter of Oleg Cassini and actress Gene Tierney. Awkwardly real-

ized, Ross' 11-inch vinyl *Tina Cassini* is most distinguished for her chicly illustrated packaging and fashion booklet,* which was in no way designed or approved by Oleg Cassini. In fact, the small Brooklyn-based toy company had approached Gene Tierney, who was no longer married to Mr. Cassini, for the rights to their daughter's identity. "Things would have turned out much better if they had consulted Tina on her actual lifestyle, and because of the poor results she has never been pleased with the doll..." said Cassini, whose daughter Tina, now with grown children of her own, lives in Paris.

Curiously, *Tina's* fashion booklet presents a dozen, enticingly-titled ensembles presented in the format of a fashion show, with a running commentary that credits the admirably unlitigious Mr.

Cassini with their design. This fashion prose, meant to be said as the model is coming down the runway, included "Did you know Oleg Cassini is a fabulous skier? And now after skiing at St. Moritz in Switzerland and all the famous slopes of Europe, he has designed the perfect ski outfit for you and Tina.!" Sold in the 1965 Sears Catalog for approximately $5.00, her fashions went for about half that. On today's secondary market, *Tina Cassini* is about $150.00, mint-in-box, including booklet. Her fashions, mint-in-box, are about $75.00.

*

*

*

*

*

ALEXANDER'S JACQUELINE

Both Princess Diana and Jackie "K-O" certainly appeal to the public in the classic Hollywood manner. Like Princess Diana, there are a variety of Jackie dolls, past and present. While most qualify as celebrity dolls, Madame Alexander's *Jacqueline*, both past and present, qualifies as a fashion superstar. Leave it to the formidable Madame to forge ahead despite a lack of endorsement

*

from the then first Lady, and turn her latest celebrity tribute into a fashion doll that was spectacular enough to be brilliantly revived 35 years later, in limited-edition, as one of the company's most precious collectibles.

Introduced in 1961, and in production for two years, *Jacqueline* consisted of a hard-plastic *Cissy* body with vinyl arms, attached to a specially sculpted, molded vinyl head. Jointed at the neck, shoulders, hips, and knees, she had a dark brown, signature page-boy hairstyle, brown sleep eyes, and high-heel ready arched feet. Her lavish wardrobe, incredibly simple in cut and line, was sumptuous in fabric and detail, much like its real-life counterpart. Originally sold for approximately $30.00, these dolls in mint-in-box condition now go for several thousand dollars; their separate ensembles for hundreds.

In 1997 Alexander's John Puzewski brought the long discontinued *Jacqueline* back to life, using the original face sculpt with a new, shapelier 21-inch vinyl body with hard plastic legs. Limited to an edition of 2,000, the doll* came with three elaborately accessorized outfits (including a jewel case full of Robert Sorel baubles) and retailed for approximately $600.00. No longer reissued, she has more than doubled in price on the secondary market. A 10-inch "shadow" *Jacqueline*, still being sold in variations of the larger doll's fashions, retails for approximately $100.00.

"She is the ultimate clothing doll," says Puzewski, who designed a wardrobe for *Jacqueline* that, like *Cissy's*, is evocative of the past but very much of the present. Unlike his lavishly whimsical MACouture line for *Cissy*, *Jacqueline's* designs are "very, very understated...what I did was go through the books about what Jackie wore and redesigned it, if possible, even more cinematically."

The other big difference in this *Jacqueline* is in the painting of her face, and its integration with the all-important coiffure. Both were accomplished, as with *Cissy*, by hair and make-up master Mathu Anderson. "The sculpt can look

64

*

many different ways," says Puzewski. "It is all in the interpretation. I knew Mathu was really inspired because it took him just three days to complete the new *Jacqueline's* look. The hair is amazing in itself. Standing alone without the doll, you can tell who it belongs to!" It is a pixie paean to Mr. Kenneth, who did much of Jackie's landmark 1960's hair, along with (appropriately) the hair for the film *Valley of the Dolls.* As to any actual resemblance to the real Jackie, Puzewski shares his memories of fitting her for the dress she wore to her daughter Caroline's wedding. Then an assistant to designer Carolina Herrera, it was Puzewski's sketch of Caroline's wedding dress that graced the *New York Times.* "The thing that struck me most was that she was human..."

*

John Puzewski's original sketch for 1997 *Jacqueline's* projected wardrobe includes several items that did not make the final collection. Originally designed in beige, *Jacqueline's* Chanel-style suit was all too predicably changed to pink and, even more predictably, caused sensitive collectors some consternation.

Peck Aubrey's Paper Doll representing Alexander's original Jacqueline, mirrors the doll's naive, yet sophisticated appeal.

66

BOB MACKIE

This special Limited Edition lithograph of the Bob Mackie Barbie® doll was created by Mr. Mackie especially for this evening, February 12, 1990, as a gift to commemorate Mattel Toys "World of Imagination." Edition limited to 1,000.

In the designer-label crazed 1970s, Bob Mackie stands out for dressing both divas and dolls. The Hollywood diva that brought him major recognition was Cher, and in 1976, New York's Mego Corporation introduced both *Cher* and then-husband *Sonny Bono*, as 12-inch vinyl, multi-jointed fashion dolls. They were the most popular in a series of 70's celebrity fashion dolls introduced by Mego, including *Diana Ross, Farrah Fawcett, Kate Jackson, Lynda Carter, Suzanne Somers,* and "*The Captain*" and *Toni Tenille*. All compellingly sculpted into curious likenesses, the dolls are perfect mannequins for the incredible Bob Mackie outfits designed for the *Sonny* and *Cher* dolls.

Primarily window-boxed in either purple or green packaging, four of the hardest to find Mackie creations, "Velvet Lady," "Stormy Weather," "Mother Goose," and "Liberty Bell" came in black window boxes. *Cher's* leopard-spotted "Laverne" ensemble came on a card, as did some other Mackie designs, as well as those non-Mackie creations meant for the other dolls. This mini-myriad of Bob Mackie masterpieces is a dazzling reflection of a (to put it diplomatically) unique decade.

Beautifully made, these ensembles include a terrific "catalog of Sonny and Cher's designer collection," as well as a "magic mirror card for *Cher's* dressing room playset,"* in each box. An incredible 32 ensembles are listed in *Cher's* section of the fold-out color catalog; an additional six covering the harder to find *Sonny*, making him one of the few "designer" male dolls ever mass-manufactured. The Mego dolls' many joints tend to chemically meld into each other, ruining the clothing if it is left on them. The dressing room*, in 70's shades of turquoise, sand and taupe (presaging the post-modern 80's "Santa Fe" style) is the perfect place, along with an even rarer "Sonny & Cher Travel Trunk," to keep these glittering treasures.

The Mego celebrity dolls sold for about $15.00 on the primary market, their boxed and carded costumes going for between $5.00 and $10.00. Today, highly collectible as amusing icons of the revived interest in 1970's style, the dolls go for upwards of $150.00 (Linda Carter's rare

*

*

*

*

*

*

Wonder Woman twin nemesis *Nubia* going for as much as $500.00, mint-in-box!) and the outfits, mint-in-box, start at $75.00, depending on their rarity and design popularity. Due to his recent demise, *Sonny's* mint-in-box doll is currently about $175.00, compared to *Cher's* $150.00 price tag, putting *Sonny* on a par with the rare *Growing Hair Cher*, who also goes for about $175.00, mint-in-box. *Cher's* terrific dressing room, which I purchased down the street (at what is now a Starbucks) for about $10.00 in the 1980s, now goes for about $150.00, mint-in-box. The rare, brilliantly stickered travel trunk is about $250.00.

In the late 1980s, charming southerner Mackie went into a highly successful agreement with Mattel to design a daz-

z l i n g line of BARBIE® dolls. Though qualifying (much like his actual collections) as Vegas showstoppers, the first doll in the line, a glamorously sequined BARBIE® goddess,* with a decidedly "Madonna-like hairdo" (to paraphrase Auntie Mame), harkened to the costume-crossover mentality of the 70's Mego dolls. The ultimate example of BARBIE® doll's "platinum" 1980s period, this spectacular doll, which sold originally for about $150.00, has accrued, in mint-in-box condition, to about $500.00. The stunning debut of this doll (and the elaborately costumed doll lines that continue to follow*) paved the way for Mackie's continued success in the designer fashion doll world, including several other non-Mattel dolls now on the market. These include an 18-inch porcelain fashion doll, "*Marissa*, the world's most beautiful model"*, that is available from Franklin Heirloom Dolls for about $200.00.

NOLAN MILLER

Another charming southerner, Nolan Miller toiled for years in Hollywood, designing everything from Loretta Young's famous television entrance ensembles, to Eva Gabor's Green Acres negligees, where he (with the divine Eva's assistance) managed to bring sublime chic to the chickenyard! In the 1980s he attained major recognition by designing the over-the-top concoctions on televisions *Dynasty*. With ingenious mannequins like Joan Collins and Linda Evans to interpret his vision of "post-modern" Hollywood glamour, Mr. Miller brought status-quo fashion to style-starved television viewers the world over. Like his coworker Collins, Miller jumped on the promotional bandwagon big time. Naturally this led to a line of dolls, albeit an obscure one. Being told that Mr. Miller would not be available for an interview for this book, I came across something I wrote in 1984 (in the pre-Conde Nast version of *Details* magazine):

Nolan Miller has taken over the crucial job left vacant by the passing of Edith Head. He sheathes our goddesses in glamour, who might otherwise resemble a pack of tasteless little, and not so little, actresses. He is well qualified and inherently understands the functional traditions of Hollywood design — a little waistline, a lot of cleavage, an occasional leg, and tons of beads. Mr. Miller is presently permeating the style-starved sticks with a myriad of Dynasty licensees, with varying degrees of success. One of these happens to be dolls, which I previewed one morning at the Dyanson Gallery. Arriving late, I was reassured by the sight of the appealingly handsome and silvery Mr. Miller, standing a tad uncomfortably amid a media blitz. Sipping champagne and orange juice in a crystal glass from a sumptuous breakfast buffet, Mr. Miller momentarily gazed at the stunning Hurrell portraits of Hollywood's glamour legends that adorned the walls. As a child he adulated these icons. Now

he dresses them. Nolan prefers live models. The best he could say for these dolls was that they don't talk back.

The Dynasty doll clothes presented many problems; from restrictions in working in scale, to those imposed by the manufacturer, World Doll Co., who smeared an uncharacteristic smile on Alexis' face. "I did insist they put Joan ($125.00) in a red dress. You've got to put a tart in a red dress." Smiling laconically, Mr. Miller added, "Perhaps I should say I insisted *"Alexis* be in a red dress..." Mid-anecdote, Mr. Miller's face turned ashen as, in chagrined horror, he noted that Krystle's $10,000.00 gown was too short. He conferred with a ferret-like toy exec about correcting the mistake. As I departed, Mr. Miller was fending off a whole pack of toy-ferrets beckoning him to the toy factory in Brooklyn. I am pleased to report that he opted for his workrooms in Hollywood. And if Nolan Miller does make the frequent field trip, who can blame him if it is, proverbially, to the bank...

These original Dynasty dolls, sold through the Dyanson Gallery, came in both 11½-inch and 14-inch porcelain versions. The smaller dolls, apparently for the sake of promotion, sold for $10,000. The larger, less detailed versions went for $125.00. Obscure to the max, I would have to say that today they would be worth whatever the market will support. In other words, if you have any of these dolls, hold on to them. Eventually everything becomes appreciated again, even the 1980s!

Private couturier Miller, who also hawks licensed jewelry on QVC, currently has a ravishingly realized 11½-inch vinyl doll* from Mattel which ideally resembles his close pal and doll maven, Candy Spelling. It sells on the primary market for approximately $135.00.

TRAVILLA

The late William Travilla (whose screen credit was simply "Travilla") started out in the 1940s doing sketches for studio designers scouring The Western Costume Company, where he was employed, for ensembles that could be recycled into "B" films. Eventually becoming the sartorial protégé' of popular 40's star Ann Sheridan, Travilla's great gift for transposing glamour led him to a long running contract with 20th Century Fox, and a legendary working (and personal) relationship with blonde icon Marilyn Monroe. In addition to designing most of Monroe's major costumes, (including her astonishing attire in *Gentlemen Prefer Blondes*), and the inevitable *Loretta Young Show* entrance sweepers, Travilla also designed the now classic costumes in the film *Valley of the Dolls*.

Sitting by his pool some years ago, the delightfully forthright designer told me he was asked to play the designer in *Valley of the Dolls*, Ted Casablanca, but "sensibly" declined. As for that film, he seemed mystified at its ongoing popularity. "I just didn't think it was a very good movie, and a lot of unhappiness happened from the movie. The producer and the director both died. Sharon Tate got killed by Manson. Judy Garland started to do the film and was canned in three days — pitiful. Susan Hayward is gone. It's kind of frightening. It's like a bad luck film. Jacqueline Susann is gone. Patty Duke went on to become president of the Screen Actors Guild (laughter)..."

Mr. Travilla was just as candid about his Hollywood design peers. "I've not mixed around with fashion people. Adrian and Irene were great designers. I can't say that much for Edith (Head), because she was really a stylist and not a designer. That to me is not inspirational. But she had a hell of a great career and is very well-loved in Hollywood."

It would be fascinating to hear Travilla's opinion on Mattel's recent 11½-inch vinyl Marilyn Monroe series' ravishingly recognizable (if uncredited) appropriations of his designs from *The Seven Year Itch* and *Gentleman Prefer Blondes,** along with Franklin Mint's ongoing series of 19-inch porcelain Marilyn mannequins, also featuring similar sizzling schmatas, in addition to a gold lamé one designed, but never used, for *Gentlemen Prefer Blondes.** Another Travilla "tribute," from *There's No Business Like Show Business**, is also featured on a different, 19-inch porcelain *Franklin Mint Marilyn.** The current primary market prices for the Mattel Marilyn dolls are each approximately $65.00 at K-Mart. Franklin Mint's Marilyn dolls are the usual five payments of $40.00 per doll, with the secondary market on these costumed figurines a complete mystery to me.

*

*

*

HELEN ROSE

The late, and often underrated, Hollywood designer Helen Rose eventually picked up the legendary Adrian's mantle at MGM studios, after that designer declared screen glamour dead and went into business for himself. Responsible for overseeing MGM's opulent costume productions, which were often commissioned to extravagant freelance designers like Irene Sharaff (not to be confused with the single monikered, previously mentioned Irene), Rose specialized in the more "realistic" looks that had taken precedence in the postwar period. At MGM, this meant making luscious Elizabeth Taylor look credibly chic, a task Rose successfully took to heart, even designing Taylor's first (along with Grace Kelly's only) wedding gown. Whereas it was Sharaff who would design Taylor's 1960's cross-over, cocktail party creations in Fox's *Cleopatra*, it was Rose who brought the goddess dazzlingly "down-to-earth" in fascinating 50's MGM films like *Cat On A Hot Tin Roof*. The white chiffon cocktail dress (originally designed in red) that Taylor wore for much of that opus became one of the most "knocked-off" dresses (in every color!) of that decade.

Two of Rose's most memorable Taylor designs, the aforementioned cocktail dress (along with a less memorable black sheath from *Butterfield 8*), were adequately recreated (and uncredited) on a beautifully sculpted 11½-inch vinyl doll of the actress*. Sold in wonderfully realized editions (one for *Butterfield 8*, another for *Cat On A Hot Tin Roof*, and possibly a *Father of the Bride*), sometime in the mid 1980s (the box has no date) for approximately $25.00; today, mint-in-box, these relatively rare dolls go for around $250.00. The large window box featuring "Elizabeth Taylor as she appears in..." is credited to "Tristar," the copyright saying "1960 Metro Goldwyn Mayer, INC. and Afton-Linebrook Productions," which is also repeated on a peel-off sticker on the otherwise unmarked doll's back.

In 1988, a similar, less appealing edition of the Elizabeth Taylor dolls was released with Ted Turner's name replacing Tristar's, reflecting both a corporate and a quality change. The black box became white, the black sheath turned into a white slip under a poorly concocted white peignoir. The white cocktail dress from *Cat On A Hot Tin Roof* was also pictured on the box, along with a dreadful rendition of the wedding gown from *Father of the Bride**. (An exquisite version of this gown appears on page 120, as well as a rendition of Rose's real life wedding gown for Grace Kelly on page 123) All were sold separately, dressed on the doll. The doll and her costumes are not nearly as detailed or as dramatic as the earlier edition. Originally around $15.00, in mint condition this version goes for around $150.00.

Far more evocative of the gowns, if not the star, is an ingenious Alexander homage in their now legendary 1996 collection called "Hollywood Classics," wherein (although her movie likeness is used) only Miss Taylor's screen characters are represented. The adorably evocative 10-inch vinyl "Maggie the Cat"* (see page 107) wears Rose's famous white cocktail ensemble. These dolls, which originally sold for about $150.00, were produced only briefly. This fact, coupled with Taylor's reticence to license her extraordinary looks, makes for very few Elizabeth Taylor representations (named or otherwise) on the market, rendering these exquisite examples extremely precious.

GIVENCHY

Considered one of the greatest living couturiers (albeit retired at his former fashion house), Hubert de Givenchy owes much of his fame in America to the late film icon Audrey Hepburn, in whose films he designed clothing so classic as to establish both actress and designer forever in the universal (and that includes the studio) hall of fashion fame. Although a celebrated couturier, Givenchy had to play hard ball in the 1950s in order to take credit for his movie designs. His problems were brought on by the aforementioned Edith Head, who often "shopped" designs when appropriate, while appropriating credit for the productions' costumes overall, due to her own contractual position.

From her American film debut in *Roman Holiday*, Audrey Hepburn became a fashion sensation, as did anything she wore. Since much of what she wore, both on and offscreen, was Givenchy, he became understandably peeved

*

when Head got credit in the reams of editorial copy generated by one of the most fashionable film stars to ever grace the screen. Eventually both designers appropriately shared credit for many of Hepburn's most stylish films, most notably the landmark Paramount musical *Funny Face*. Another landmark Hepburn film, Paramount's *Breakfast At Tiffany's*, showcases the actress at her gamine cum sophisticate best, in dazzling Givenchy designs that remain refreshingly chic to this day.

Another celebrity who guarded her image carefully, it was just prior to Hepburn's death in 1993 that dolls in her *My Fair Lady* likeness were produced by Ashton Drake. In 1996 Mattel also introduced *My Fair Lady* character dolls, wearing intricately realized uncredited designs based on Cecil Beaton's astounding costumes for the film musical which starred Hepburn. The dolls themselves bore a vague likeness to the actress*, who was the proportional antithesis of a *Barbie* doll. For 1998, Mattel is about to release a celebrity version of Audrey Hepburn,* dressed in an uncredited "homage" Givenchy black gown from *Breakfast At Tiffany's*. Two more Givenchy designs, a sophisti-

*

cated "cat mask" ensemble,* and an inevitable pink party dress, (both seen in the film), come separately boxed. Givenchy's famous black, fringed day ensemble with huge hat,* originally to be sold separately, may be sold dressed on the doll.*

Long awaited by legions of Audrey Hepburn fans the world over, the doll is (at least in photographs) somewhat of a down-scaled version of the "Eliza Dolittle" editions. Whereas the *My Fair Lady* Eliza character dolls had rooted eyelashes,* this doll does not. An across-the-board poll had many mistaking her for another 98' Mattel celebrity offering, soap superstar Susan Lucci* (who on the following page, with fashionable Cruella de Vil* as stepmother, makes a perfect step sis for Eliza's *Cinderella*!)

Mattel is promising a series of Audrey Hepburn dolls, and consequent costumes (imagine her mod masterpiece *Two For The Road*!), all of which, despite any ambiguity, are sure to be popular. The series is called "The Audrey Hepburn Collection," with the dressed doll retailing for about $65.00 and the boxed costumes around $40.00. Hopefully no shortages will give collectors Golightly's infamous "mean reds," keeping them from their long-awaited daydream of having a perfectly chic little Audrey of their own.

*

*

*

*

*

77

EDITH HEAD

Like her successful male peers, Edith Head knew how to make sometimes less than anatomically perfect actresses look not just simply divine, but downright sexy. This combined with an innate genius for self-promotion (and a keen ability to delegate), kept her working at the top of her field for six decades.

An eight-time Academy Award winner who worked on over 1,100 films, Head proved as adaptable to the cruel whims of fashion as to the brutally changing studio system. An androgynous, ageless figure, she created a persona part school marm, part elf. Her curious demeanor became familiar to baby boomers (and their moms) on Art Linkletter's popular daytime television *House Party*, where for several decades she would scold people on their inappropriate attire, making light of their foibles while offering instant make-over suggestions. Remembered today as Hollywood's most accoladed designer, Head brought to the screen, throughout her long tenure, a genius for consistently capturing classic style combined with classy sensuality.

In 1997, the L.L. Knickerbocker Company, Inc. entered an agreement with Universal Studios Consumer Products Group to recreate certain Head fashions in a collectible porcelain doll line. Knickerbocker then commissioned doll artist Robert Tonner to create the dolls, which were not to represent individual actresses but (probably to save more copyright costs and headaches) merely suggest the aura of a generic Hollywood star. In this sense the dolls are similar to Mel Odom's *Gene*® (see page 80), however lacking Gene®'s distinctly ungeneric mystique.

Formerly a designer at Bill Blass for fifteen years, Mr. Tonner has proven an adept politician since entering the fashion doll world in the early 1990s, having established (much like Head herself) an adoring market. Despite the raves in Mr. Tonner's press kit, however, I find these porcelain mannequins to resemble poorly turned out transsexuals; their strip (as opposed to full-cap) wigs particularly problematic.

These five, 16½-inch porcelain dolls from the same sculpt, with different painting and hair, represent five of Head's films, including *She Done Him Wrong** (which qualifies, like all but one, as a "cross-over costume"). Three other offerings from more obscure films, *The Big Broadcast,** *This Way Please**, and the retro rehash *Gable and Lombard** are beautifully realized, however the purely costume contribution from *The Heiress** has the look of a lamp-shade. The L.L. Knickerbocker Co. is known for their high quality, and these dolls reflect their approximately $175.00 price tag.Two other, more evocative dolls pay unoffi-cial homage to Edith Head's legacy. One, inevitably from Franklin-Mint, is a hauntingly fragile 19-inch porcelain fig-urine of Marilyn Monroe from *All About Eve,** wearing Edith Head's (uncredited) white satin jacquard gown, and a fluffily faux, white full-length fur coat; with a pri-mary price of approximately $200.00. Another of Alexander's 10-inch vinyl dolls, from their 1996 collection, features "Angela Vickers" (as portrayed by Elizabeth Taylor) from Paramount's *A Place In The Sun*, wearing Head's famous lilac tulle "prom" dress that became a Seventh Avenue sen-sation. Most esoteric is a prototype 10-inch Alexander doll based on Tippi Hedren in *The Birds,** wearing a clas-sic Chanel-style suit like the one sup-plied by Head for the film, and acces-sorized by feathered black birds. Some humorless buyers complained and the line, which also featured a homage to *Psycho*'s Janet Lee (in the shower, wrapped in a Bates Motel towel), was cancelled.

79

GENE®

When I spoke with Oleg Cassini, he understandably expressed dismay over the name Gene being used for a doll representing a 1940's movie star, feeling it seemed all too obviously an unrenumerated play on the name of his late former wife Gene Tierney.

Having been in on illustrator Mel Odom*'s 15½-inch vinyl *Gene*® doll since practically her inception, (and one of the first to write about her editorially), I am also the first to realize she doesn't officially qualify as a designer fashion doll. However, particularly since I have expressed my disappointment at the first edition Edith Head dolls, I will qualify *Gene* as a designer doll in spirit; elegantly evocative of the golden age of Hollywood that Head so beautifully captured. In fact, *Gene*®'s original three costume designers, Timothy Albert*, Doug James*, and Tim Kennedy* (who carefully stipulated what would be a "real" ensemble as opposed to a "movie costume"), are all well-established, extremely talented costume designers. Also of note is Laura Meisner,* who has designed some of *Gene*®'s most popular ensembles, and Dolly Cippola, who reinterprets the prototype creations into those mass-produced for the public.

As realized by Ashton-Drake, (known previously for their emphasis on porcelain baby dolls, my favorite being a toddler wielding a roll of toilet paper), *Gene*® took the doll world (and apparently Ashton-Drake) by storm in 1995. Her exquisite coupling of concept and execution has made *Gene*® one of the most exciting fashion dolls currently on the primary market. Unlike the majority of today's generically wide-eyed, toothily smiling 11½-inch fashion dolls, *Gene*®'s sophisticated mystique is rooted (as are her hair and eyelashes) in the increasingly popular tradition of the hard plastic fashion dolls of the 1950s.

Gene®'s larger size allows for finer detailing of costumes, and her initial clothing

collections, which are now beginning to be discontinued, are sure to become highly collectible. This seems particularly adept now that Ashton-Drake seems to have switched its design emphasis on *Gene®'s* clothing from the original professionals to assorted competitions among students and collectors. Conceived by doll scholar John Darcy Noble as a well-intentioned way of fostering new talent, the idea seems to have taken some kind of corporate twist, and the results are visible in *Gene®'s* latest collection. It will be interesting to see how this affects the doll's evolution. While *Gene®* is sold dressed for about $80.00 and her costumes for approximately $40.00, the secondary market price on the first discontinued "Premiere" *Gene®* doll is now $800.00!

*

Smart Set
(inspired by
Norman
Norell)

*

*

Blonde Lace
(inspired by
Marlene
Dietrich)

Mandarin
Mood
(inspired by
Madame
Gres)

*

Embassy
Luncheon

81

*

Ransom in Red

*

El Morocco

*

Gold Sensation
(inspired by Mel
Odom)

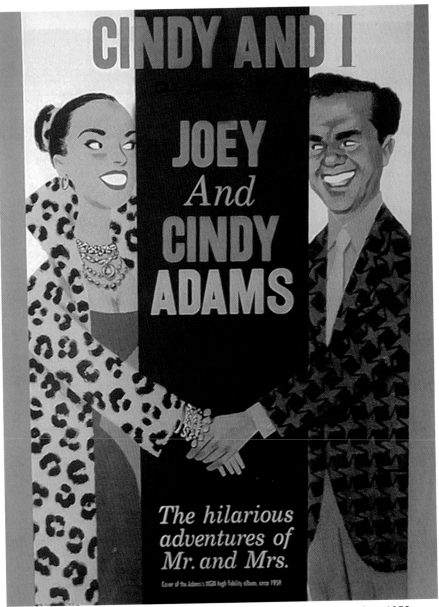

The cover of the Adams' MGM high fidelity *Cindy and I* album, circa 1959.

One of the world's leading celebrity commentators, born Goddess (and former "Miss Brooklyn Bagel") Cindy Adams also has the distinction of being one of the world's rarest celebrity fashion dolls. While not designer-endorsed, Horsman's 1958 limited-edition *Cindy and I* dolls are a landmark in sophisticated fashion doll imagery.

"The problem is the doll's face has never changed and mine has," laughed Adams, sitting amid the royal splendor of the Far East in her new penthouse above Park Avenue. (Indeed, while the dolls' features remain frozen in time, their namesake has since youthfully softened.) Cindy's all-knowing eyes lit up when she told me

Cindy Adams

about her little likenesses, which she said were manufactured to promote her husband, beloved comedian Joey Adams' best selling chronicle of their marriage, *Cindy and I*. "There was a lot of publicity about us and one night in some restaurant the head of this toy company (Horsman) came up and said to Joey, "She's a doll, your wife...."

The next thing she knew, Madame Adams was working with Horsman's talented artists and designers. They captivatingly recreated her ravishing face and distinctive hairdo, best described by Mr. Adams on the linear notes of the MGM record album of "Cindy and I" – "My Cindy is easily recognized by her patent leather haircomb. It's jet black, parted in the middle, and pulled back sleek and tight. I don't know if she combs it with an iron or paints it on. I finally discovered why she never shuts her mouth. Her hair is on too tight!"

Cindy's wardrobe at this time was designed principally by Trigere, Stravapolous, and Halston. "We wore froufrou stuff then. It wasn't a casual look. I wore only red, white, or black, big jewelry, and industrial strength eye makeup." Horsman's clever designers saw to it that "the doll and I dressed alike...she was dressy, with <u>lots</u> of clothes and accessories, lots of 'diamonds'...all dolls then were blonde and blue-eyed. My doll had big black eyes."

Never a doll collector previously, Cindy had been unimpressed with the "big baby dolls that cried mama" in her own childhood. She took one look at her dramatically different namesake, however, and "I was like a kid again!" The *Cindy and I* dolls were released in a limited quantity, as an upscale promotion for both Joey's book and Horsman's elaborate line of non-celebrity *Cindy* dolls, which had been introduced the previous year. Manufactured with the standard *Cindy* 10-1/2-inch and 18-inch vinyl bodies, and specially designed heads and packaging, the *Cindy and I* doll debuted at The New York City Toy Fair in 1958, with a lavish promotion featuring Cindy in person. "I was like a seal in a cage, flapping my flippers — I'm always promoting something!" said Cindy, as she casually hoisted a huge bottle of her perfume, "Gossip".

Noted doll scholar and preservationist Laura Meisner is particularly taken by these rare *Cindy* dolls: "For me, dolls represent everything that society, at a given time, finds important. Especially fashion dolls, who represent not only the appropriate attire of a given era but the appropriate female attitude, which gives them great historical merit...These *Cindy's* look nothing like the original *Cindy* Horsman doll. The features are decidedly adult. Unlike most fashion dolls of the period, this version of *Cindy* is ultra-sophisticated and extremely cosmetic. The brows are penciled, and not feathered. Though the body is typical, the head is from a different mold. Most brunette dolls of the period had dark brown hair. This one has ink black hair. I find her to be, much like her namesake, rare and absolutely fascinating!"

Due to the doll's rarity, a mint-in-the-box *Cindy and I* doll would be hard to appraise at a dollar value, putting her into the priceless category.

What would Hollywood be without GOSSIP?!

Sensibly stashed away in one of Mrs. Adams temple-like closets, this 10½-inch *Cindy* is perfectly preserved. The *Cindy & I* logo on the tag identifies Horsman's promotional doll and separates it from the company's popular line of *Cindy* dolls, which started production the previous year.

BARBIE®

While Americans went designer name crazy during the 1970s, due to budget problems Mattel (usually the first to reflect such trends) didn't catch up until 1984, with the introduction of a lavish line of ball gowns credited to international designer Oscar de la Renta, who this year has an entirely new 11½-inch vinyl Mattel doll*, which sells exclusively at Bloomingdale's for $89.00.

The first four opulent de la Renta ballgowns, released in 1984, were called "From the collection of Oscar de la Renta for BARBIE®, COLLECTOR SERIES V"*. Apropros to nothing, the second sumptuous series, released the next year, are "From the collection of Oscar de la Renta for BARBIE®, Collector Series VIII"*. This final collection features five gowns, one restylable into a "Dynasty"-inspired cocktail confection. Selling originally for $8.50, each mint-in-window box ensemble now goes for about $175.00.

By the 1990s, with the *BARBIE®* doll garnering international attention as a 20th century icon, Mattel began to merge with much of Seventh Avenue (and some popular European fashion houses) for a variety of *BARBIE®* dolls, many of them department store specials. Mattel does not lay claim to being the world's largest manufacturer of garments for nothing. Carefully designed by committee and beautifully manufactured, these dolls perfectly reflect the *BARBIE®* doll's tradition of idealizing the status quo. Since the secondary market on most of these dolls is still in flux, I am listing the dolls with their original, primary prices along with the approximate dates of their original release.

RULING THE READY-TO-WEAR FASHION DOLL RUNWAY / BARBIE® FROM MADISON AVENUE TO SEVENTH AVENUE

"Couture"

The Best of the Lot:
BYRON LARS *In the Limelight* BARBIE® (1996 / $80.00 - no longer on primary market) & "Cinnebar Sensation" BARBIE® (1997 / $80.00)

*

*

*

From Beautiful Bondage to Ultimate Upholstery: GIAN-FRANCO FERRE/House of Dior* BARBIE® (1995 / $170.00) & CHRISTIAN DIOR *"New Look" Anniversary** BARBIE® (1996 / $170.00)

The Best Homage To Auntie Mame: Robert Best's *Portrait in Taffeta BARBIE*®*, the premier doll in the BARBIE® Couture Collection (1997 / $135.00), Mr. Best was recently recruited by Mattel from former garmento golden boy Isaac Mizrahi's design team.

Beautifully Bourgois: *Escada BARBIE*® (1997 / $160.00)

Highly Underrated: Bill Blass BARBIE® (1997 / $160.00)

*

Nicole Miller BARBIE®, Bloomingdale's Exclusive* (1995 / $65.00), and Macy's Exclusive* (1997 / $70.00)

*

"Boutique"

Anne Klein BARBIE®, Macy's Exclusive (1996 / $70.00)

Donna Karan BARBIE®, Bloomingdale's Exclusive (1995 / $65.00)

Ralph Lauren BARBIE®, Bloomingdale's Exclusive (1997 / $80.00)

Calvin Klein BARBIE®, Bloomingdale's Exclusive (1997 / $70.00)

Released at the peak of Mattel's "platinum period" quality renaissance, *Benneton BARBIE®* (1990 / $15.00 for a doll, $10.00 for an outfit) is currently $75.00 and $50.00 respectively, on the secondary market. Released both in the U.S. and Europe, this colorful, elaborate, beautifully packaged line of Benneton *BARBIE®, Ken, Christie, Midge*, and *Kira* dolls*, and six separate outfits,* are a great compliment to that company's actual line. The incredible *Ken* ensemble is one of the few *Ken* designer outfits, or dolls, in existence. The *Benneton Ken,*᠎* mint-in-box, is now about $150.00, his separate outfit* mint-in-box is about $75.00.

BARBIE® BILLYBOY

COLLECTION

Behind and beyond *BARBIE®* doll's
fashionable 1980's comeback…

*

While *BARBIE®* doll started life under the incredibly chic supervision of Charlotte Johnson, the 1970s saw this support system, (most notably creator Ruth Handler), removed from Mattel, which went into a distinct slump. This was relieved by the *BARBIE®* doll's late 70's resurrection as disco glamour goddess. As Mattel made more money, they spent more on their cash cow *BARBIE®* doll, which by the mid-1980s was mirroring the *Dynasty* mentality of the times. Much like T.V.'s *Dynasty*, *BARBIE®* was hopelessly unhip in terms of her fashions. The brilliant Kay Thompson's credo "Think Pink" in the landmark fashion film *Funny Face*, was taken to nauseating ubiquity by Mattel's marketing department, who went so far as to copyright their own version of the color. Long gone (but far from forgotten by the growing numbers of collectors) were the subtly sophisticated hues favored by Johnson. Mattel, at this point, looked upon their doll's collectibility as a nuisance. In 1985, however, they took an unusually brilliant step, commissioning fashion artist BillyBoy* to orchestrate a corporately cutting-edge tribute to the world's most famous doll, "Barbie's New Theatre of Fashion."

A member of the so-called "demimonde" (not to be confused with Demi Moore), collector, sartorial and doll historian, and avant fashion and accessory designer Billyboy* has made many contributions to the doll world. A native of Staten Island, New York, he started collecting dolls and fashion at an early age. Regally relocating to Paris, Billyboy* networked that city's fashion elite to create "*BARBIE®*'s New Theatre of Fashion," a takeoff on the *Théatré de la Mode*, utilizing, like the original, the very best Parisian couturiers, jewelers, artists and architects.

Billyboy*'s Crown book, *BARBIE® Her Life And Times*, a delightful *BARBIE®* fashion deconstruction, thoroughly documents the "New Theatre of Fashion." A fashion booklet put out by Mattel in 1985 highlights the *BARBIE®* Billyboy* collection. With a cover painting of *BARBIE®* by Mel Odom, this small paper booklet* was distributed by Mattel as part of their touring "New Theatre of Fashion." Showcasing the one-of-a-kind haute couture *BARBIE®* fashions created for the tour, it is now quite collectible, going for about $75.00 in mint condition on today's secondary *BARBIE®* market. A similiar French *Noveau Théatre de la Mode* booklet, with a striking Rene Gruau sketch of Billyboy*'s *Noveau Theatre de la Mode BARBIE®*, goes for around $100.00 mint.

Two Billyboy* *BARBIE*® dolls resulted from this New Theatre of Fashion. The first, representing the *Noveau Théatre de la Mode*, was a 1986 European-market release. This sumptuously sophisticated, black and gold clad blonde *BARBIE*® doll* was originally about $75.00 on the secondary American market. Currently, mint-in-box, it goes for about $350.00. In 1987, an American, darkly brunette Billyboy* *BARBIE*® called *Feelin Groovy BARBIE*®,* was released on the primary market for about $25.00 at F.A.O. Schwarz, and can be had today for about $250.00, mint-in-box on the secondary market. Both sporting black sunglasses, these two are valuable designer fashion dolls because of their particular place in re-establishing the *BARBIE*® doll as a real fashion presence, as opposed to the bargain basement rendition she had become by the mid-1970s. *BARBIE*® doll's requalification as a collectible fashion icon opened up a whole new marketing mentality at Mattel, paving the way for both their fashion licenses and long anticipated collector reissues of past favorites from the 1960's "golden age".

*

*

MDVANII

Having put *BARBIE®* doll back on her fashion pedestal, Billyboy* went on to create his own line of "French Couture" dolls. *Mdvanii,* by Billyboy Couture*, made her debut in 1989. Ponderously produced on a small scale, *Mdvanii* was a "mannerist" answer to the generically produced "renaissance" fashion dolls typified by *BARBIE®*. With his usual drive and access to the best design talent in both America and Europe (*Mdvanii's* face design was overseen by Mel Odom), Billyboy* went all-out in promoting his creation at American retail venues like Bloomingdale's and FAO Schwarz.

Mdvanii's lavishly illustrated premiere catalog* describes the doll: "Mdvanii (pronounced mid-vah-knee) is a 25 centimeters high fashion doll created in Paris, France, whose exquisite high-fashion wardrobe and accessories are designed and created on Rue de la Paiz, the most famous fashion street in the world!"

"Mdvanii doll is made of a special heavy resin in a pale powdered tone evocative of 1950's glamorous make-up. Her lovely features, delicate colouring and high-fashion make-up are individually hand-painted by trained artists, giving each doll a unique nuance and an alluring one-of-a-kind expression…"

"Mdvanii is naturally and beautifully proportioned like no other fashion doll in the world. Her lithe body is a work of art, a veritable sculpture! Mdvanii doll is anatomically correct, paying homage to nature's most beautiful creation — woman!"

"She is limited to 5,000 Deluxe Edition gift sets only available from Billyboy* Toys in Paris"…

"She is hand-made and assembled in Paris, France. Mdvanii doll is labeled on the back of her head with a gold-plated metal tag with her name on it, identifying her as an original BillyBoy* Toys creation. She moves at the shoulders, thighs, and neck."

Featuring lavish color fashion sketches by Clyde Smith, one of *BARBIE®* doll's original illustrators, the 1989 catalog credits Alexandre de Paris with creating *Mdvanii's* wigs, and goes on to describe in detail the "Deluxe Edition Mdvanii Doll," "Basic 'Dress Up'able Mdvanii Doll," and "Sixteen Deluxe Edition Giftsets." along with twenty-four couture ensembles, in addition to separates and accessories. While no prices are listed in this catalog, a 1992 catalog introducing *Mdvanii's* black female friend *Dheei** listed dressed dolls priced at $350.00 to $650.00; separate outfits and accessories starting at $40.00 for a pillbox hat, and a boxed set of evening accessories ("limited to 100 examples") for $450.00. A simple black cotton sleeveless sheath, titled "Fourreau," was $145.00.

Eventually other dolls were added to the line, including two anatomically correct males. One white (*Rhogit-Rhogit*), the other black (*Zhdrick**), both "basic studs" (as they were referred to) were of ambiguous (albeit blatant) sexuality, and

96

were featured in their own black and white catalog, beautifully illustrated by Clyde Smith. Marketed with a "safe sex" theme,* the male dolls came with a condom, and in one edition their own original sculpture or painting. According to the catalog, "Both men come with an assortment of manly tattoos...ready for you to apply in the most provocative places! They both have a pierced ear for exotic earrings. *Rhogit-Rhogit* has his ear pierced on the right, *Zhdrick* on the left. Both men can wear an assortment of wigs over their butch regulation Marine haircuts. These wigs compliment their manly and exotic wardrobes which coordinate with *Mdvanii* and *Dheei's* splendidly feminine clothes." The prices of these male dolls and their elaborate presentation sets, though written in English, are listed in Francs, each basic stud going for 5,000 FF.

A 1993 September/October issue of *Barbie Bazaar* features a full-page back inside cover of a "limited edition" *Edie*, dressed and tressed *tre mod*. No price is included. The inside front and back covers of *Barbie Bazaar* throughout 1993, featuring fashionably photographed advertisements for *Mdvanii* and her fabulous friends, indicate her golden age. By the mid-90s, *Mdvanii* and her court, who were always rarefied, began to become mythic. Their oddly stiff, detached countenances, coupled with their costly couture quality, certainly contributed to their brief reign. As such, they remind me of the extremely rare, rigid, mysteriously forbidding, and anatomically correct court dolls of Marie Antoinette.

Already expensive in their first run, *Mdvanii* and company, along with her accessories and some furnishings, are on the secondary market so rarefied as to be considered priceless. Rumors recently had *Mdvanii* being resurrected by a Japanese company, giving her well-deserved myth a boost.

97

Second Edition

First Edition

These Harley's Rule More Than The Road...

I have not included the many dolls issued representing garment manufacturers. Sergio Valenti is <u>not</u>, to my knowledge, an actual designer — though the extremely rare 11½-inch vinyl black male in his signature doll line is a real find! Mr. Harley and Mr. Davidson are seminally subliminal, however, in their sartorial influence on Twentieth Century American fashion.

Mattel's two *BARBIE*® doll tributes, from 1997* and 1998,* are the perfect blend of two American legends; the former, a limited Toys R Us edition, quickly sold out and is now on the secondary market for about three times the original $60.00 price. The current "Collector Edition" also sells for $60.00 at Toys R Us.

From 1996, Alexander's fabulously frilly 10-inch *Cissette** proved unpopular with Harley-Davidson and was not produced; from 1997 an obvious compromise of the earlier, frilly *Cissette*; the saucily sensational, 10-inch faux leather clad *Cissette** is from Alexander's 1998 catalog. Both produced dolls sell for approximately $150.00.

*

*

*

99

BILLY & BOB

Two male dolls, a generation apart, qualify as fashion dolls with a (pun intended) designer bent. Both 1977's *Gay Bob* and 1997's *Billy* (no relation to Billyboy*) have wardrobes which amusingly reflect the designer-friendly "gay lifestyle" aspect of the diverse homosexual community. Stereotypical by design, both dolls can trace their origins to the gift market. *Gay Bob's* "closet" is deftly reflected in the pages of his clothing catalog*. Although the outfits were never actually produced, it is a brilliant sociological spoof of 1970's male sartorial conceits.

"I believe you have to convey a serious message with humor," said Dr. Harvey Rosenberg, discussing his 1977 creation of *Gay Bob* with me in 1997, for *Candi*, Intl. Magazine. Along with graphic artist Jennifer Anderson, Rosenberg (who off-handedly commented that he happens to be straight) wanted to illustrate that "everyone should have a right to live openly and honestly, as opposed to lying about themselves." He took a generic G.I Joe clone and added "an accurate penis and an earring in the left ear," while Jennifer created a lavish "closet" from which Bob could be liberated.

Fifty Thousand *Gay Bob* dolls were introduced in 1977, taking off in a media flash! Shown for a year, he sold out. *Gay Bob's* sociological prescience (in coming out twenty years before Ellen) created a successful fad that turned into a valued collectible. Sold originally for about $25.00, *Gay Bob* now goes, mint-in-"closet" box, for about $400.00. Toy inventor Rosenberg considers Bob "my most famous toy." The closet represented "a metaphoric space, with its own powerful message about civil rights and personal integrity."

In 1977, MGM commissioned Gizmo to come up with a prototype for a doll of the transvestite character from *The Rocky Horror Picture Show*. The result was this mercifully one-of-a-kind rooted-hair *Gay Bob*. His maquillage a mess, he is however resplendent in a feathery Bob Mackie ensemble, originally intended for Mego's *Cher*.

Unlike his more realistically crafted 12-inch predecessor *Gay Bob*, Totem's beautifully sculpted 12½-inch *Billy* isn't actually able to hold his historic, if anatomically (and politically) incorrect, appendage.

Lot's of Love

Billy

    Billy was originally conceived as a two-dimensional fashion sketch ("with a distinctly gay character") by British freelance fashion designer John McKitterick, to model creations for Jean Paul Gaultier. Friends encouraged McKitterick to come up with a three-dimensional mannequin of Billy. In 1995, a small British company was formed called F.O.B. (Friends of Billy) for that very purpose, producing a limited-edition (approximately 1,200), completely hand-crafted, 17-inch *Billy*[*] doll made from a special formula of latex rubber. He sold for approximately $300.00.

    The doll came dressed in one of twelve separate designs, including "Master Billy," "Baby Billy," "*Gay Boy Billy,*"* "Sporty *Billy,*" "Sailor *Billy,*" "Cowboy *Billy,*" "Muscle Boy *Billy,*" "Slave *Billy,*" "Army *Billy,*" "San Francisco *Billy,*" "Clone *Billy,*" and "Rubber *Billy.*" Considered an amusing curiosity in England because of his anatomically oversized genitalia, *Billy* quickly sold out when introduced in the United States. In 1997, Totem, International brought a vinyl, 12-inch *Billy* to the U.S., incorrectly tagging the doll as "The first out and proud gay doll."

    One of the most beautifully sculpted and manufactured vinyl dolls ever produced, Totem's European-made 12-inch *Billy* comes dressed in one of four incredibly detailed ensembles representing a San Francisco clone *Billy*, a leather Master *Billy*, and a Cowboy and Sailor *Billy*. A *Wall Street Billy,** though included in the original packaging, was not to my knowledge produced. Obviously inspired sartorially by The Village People, *Billy's* huge genitalia, along with an unturning head and the countenance of a youthful Ed Asner, made him more of a gift-market curiosity than an ongoing fashion doll collectible. *Billy's* bulge is, while a brilliant novelty, a shortcoming for fashion doll collectors in terms of his fashions' "improper" fit.

    Designer McKitterick, now devoting himself fulltime to *Billy's* success, said in a 1997 interview with me for *Doll Journal*: "I started in 1992 and I've gone from not knowing anything about dolls whatsoever to actually sculpting dolls, working in factories with dolls, learning about painting faces of dolls, etc...I'm now beginning to understand what doll collecting is about - buying this and that for the doll, and playing with it."

    Tirelessly promoting *Billy* as an upbeat gay image (as opposed to those who take him literally, as a heathen toyboy), McKitterick and partner Juan Ortiz introduced a boyfriend for *Billy*, named *Carlos*, in 1998. A line of clothing, including the first four costumes, was realized separately. Fetish/sportswear designer Ramond Dragon* has also manufactured a limited line of form-fitting garments for both dolls. Touting safe sex and other rainbow-image slogans, *Billy's* next hurdle remains in overcoming his proportional problems in looking anything but ridiculous in (or for that matter out of) the all important fashions. Hooking up with Tom of Finland for a mini-collection of their sportswear-line might be a positive way of compromising *Billy's* cross-marketability, with Tom's classic appeal to mollify those humorless souls who would kill this delightful doll messenger.

Recently, a glitzy charity promotion, "Lifebeat - The Music Industry Fights AIDS," prompted McKitterick to network his many connections in the international fashion industry, and a variety of one-of-a-kind, designer *Billy* dolls were auctioned after being displayed in the Fifth Avenue shop windows of the fashionable British men's designer Paul Smith*.I'm informed by Mr. Ortiz that *Billy* has since been signed by a licensing agent, and a mass-manufactured line of (as yet unspecified) designer clothing, along with a new addition (also unspecified) to the doll line, will be introduced next year in Europe and possibly the United States. Because of his current fashion flux, *Billy* (who is sold dressed for about $40.00, costumes for about $15.00) is a question mark in terms of the secondary market, where he is often sold for primary prices.

KNOCK IT OFF

Fashion pays constant homage to itself/here are some ravishing reinterpretations…

PICNIC SET

(without doll) #967 — Checked gingham shirt with blue denim jeans, tailored with zipper fly. Wedge shoes and amusing straw hat. Picnic basket to carry the fish Barbie caught with her pole!
Complete set, $2.50

#967

BRADFORD SAMUELS

Grass roots Haute Couture…

In the last decade, the world of dolls has grown and evolved incredibly. It includes a wider and more diverse spectrum of both product and collectors than perhaps any other collectible genre. The doll market of the 1990s is as imaginative as it is creative, keeping marketing people on their toes, and toy corporations on the defensive. The powerful secondary market now features vintage dolls alongside incredibly restyled and recreated ones.

This marvelous myriad of individually created, hybrid dolls are by far best represented by doll artist Bradford Samuels' exquisitely realized renditions of real haute couture. As reflections of the real world, dolls are intrinsically in costume. By so intricately recreating haute couture, Samuels reflects for the doll world what haute couture represents for the real world; rarefied, opulent fantasy.

"All my dolls are based on haute couture, from 1947's New Look to the early 1960s. Most are in tribute to the great mid-20th Century European designers, including Balenciaga, Dior, Deffes, and Fath," Samuels told me recently, adding "The fashion of the 50s and early 60s is what makes me tick. The purity of Balenciaga, the sophistication of Dior…are from what I draw my inspiration. My own doll creations are a respectfully loving homage to these original designers."

A veteran of both the beauty and interior design industries, since 1996 Samuels toils full-time creating these virtually one-of-a-kind mannequins. Attention to minutae being his strongest attribute, he even manages to recreate a french twist in scale to the 11½-inch vinyl doll. When I asked why not a larger, less difficult size, Samuels laughed, "It's some masochistic attraction to this one scale. I love the way clothes hang on a fashion model body. I modify the doll's body severely to get the proportions I need. So severely, the clothes have to stay on (permanently). When I use closures I am not happy with the fit. I want them to look like they are holding in their breath, in order to fit in the garment."

"I work with preowned fashion dolls, unpopular ones from 1976. I love the idea of saving a doll destined for the dustbin. I strip the paint and hair, repaint faces down to the iris of the eyes. I reroot the hair and lashes, and rearticulate the dolls' bodies and appendages to show the outfits off to best advantage," continued Samuels.

A popular and respected figure at doll conventions around the country, artist Samuels does between twenty and thirty dolls a year, each of which averages from ten to forty hours of work, including resculpting and complete handsewing. His privileged clientele pay between $195.00 and $795.00 for individual dolls, none of which have so far reappeared on the market.

These divinely detailed, haute couture mannequins harken to the original *Théatré de la Mode*, coming full circle from designer original, to the most elegant post-designer homage imaginable.

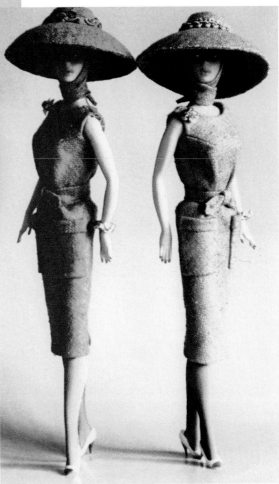

LINGERIE

Scintillating subtext, beneath the valley of designer dolls…

John Puzewski -- *Cissy* Lingerie Trunk

John Puzewski -- *Cissy* Lingerie Trunk

Timothy Albert — *Forget Me Not*

Tim Kennedy — *Pin-Up* & *The Kiss*

Jay E.Watkins &
Edward Roberts

NIGHTY-NEGLIGEE SET

(without doll) #965
Luxurious full-length
tricot gown. Grecian
bodice with
embroidered flower.
Matching peignoir of
finely tucked tricot
with embroidered
pocket. Toy stuffed
dog for Barbie's bed.
The set. $3.00

#965

Charlotte Johnson

#973

**FLORAL
PETTICOAT**

(without doll) #921
Crisp nylon sheer
petticoat, all-over
embroidered with
pastel floral design
and matching
panties. Strapless
bra, vanity mirror,
comb, brush set.
Complete.
$1.25

#921

Billyboy*

BRIDES

No runway show is complete without them...

Jay E.Watkins & Edward Roberts

Charlotte Johnson

John Puzewski

#987

ORANGE BLOSSOM®
(without doll) #987
Barbie blossoms out for a wedding or graduation
party in a buttercup yellow sheath frosted
with an embroidered sheer nylon overskirt.
Veiled tulle hat, white shoes and a bouquet
spring posies complete the pretty picture.
The set, $2.50

Charlotte Johnson

Charlotte Johnson

Vera Wang & Charlotte
Johnson for BARBIE®

Madame Alexander
Vintage Bride

Alexander Doll Company's
Father of the Bride; gown
originally designed by
Helen Rose

MA COUTURE Brides designed
by John Puzewski

Vera Wang

Doug James &
Laura Meisner

122

Helen Rose for
Princess Grace.

Timothy Albert for *Gene*®

Jacqueline Bouvier Brides

Bob Mackie *Empress Bride*

Credits:

Cover Photo courtesy of Alexander Doll Company / Page 1 Photo by Beauregard Houston-Montgomery / Page 3 Photo by Jacob Getz / Pages 4-5 Clyde Smith illustrations for Barbie, Mdvanni, and Gene, courtesy of Mattel, Billyboy*, and Ashton-Drake / Page 6 Photo by Beauregard Houston-Montgomery / Page 7 Photo by Lynton Gardner / Page 8 Photo courtesy of Alexander Doll Company / Page 9 Photo courtesy of Franklin Mint / Page 10 Photo courtesy of "Theatre de la Mode", Rizzoli/Metropolitan Museum of Art / Page 11 Photo of Jacques Heim mannequin courtesy of "Theatre de la Mode", Rizzoli/Metropolitan Museum of Art ; photos courtesy of Alexander Doll Company, Ashton-Drake / Page 12 Photo by Teddy Piaz ; label courtesy of "Howdy Do" / Page 13 Photos and artwork courtesy of Effanbee / Pages 14-15 Photos courtesy of Polly and Pam Judd / Page 16 Photo by Beauregard Houston-Montgomery / Page 17 Photo by Ande' Whyland / Page18 Photo courtesy of Alexander Doll Company / Page 19 sketch by John Puzewski / Page 20 Photo by Beauregard Houston-Montgomery / Page 21 Sketch by John Puzewski ; Photo courtesy of Alexander Doll Company / Page 22 Photo for Bloomingdale's by Chris DeGray; photo courtesy of Alexander Doll Company / Page 23 Photo courtesy of Alexander Doll Company / Page 24 Photo by Ande' Whyland ; sketch by John Puzewski / Pages 25-29 Photos courtesy of Alexander Doll Company / Pages 30-31 Photo by Ande' Whyland / Pages 32-33 Sketches and photo courtesy of Mattel; photo of Charlotte Johnson courtesy of Mr. & Mrs.Tanabe and Barbie Bazaar / Page 34 Photo by Beauregard Houston-Montgomery / Page 35 Images courtesy of Hallmark, Peck-Aubrey, Mattel; photo by Beauregard Houston-Montgomery / Pages 36-37 Photos by Ande' Whyland; sketches courtesy of Louis Marx & Company / Pages 38-39 Photos by Beauregard Houston-Montgomery / Page 40 Editorial photo of Pucci domed Braniff air hostess courtesy of Life Magazine, circa 1965 / Pages 42-43 Twiggy images courtesy of Mattel and Barbie Bazaar; package photos by Beauregard Houston-Montgomery; Twiggy doll courtesy of John Darcy Noble / Pages 46-47 Package photos by Beauregard Houston-Montgomery / Page 48 Photos by Steven Mays / Page 50 Photo of Vivienne Westwood Life Ball Barbie by Lukas Dostal ; photo courtesy of Alexander Doll Company / Page 51 Photo of Catherine Walker by Tim Graham / Page 52 Photos courtesy of Franklin Mint / Page 53 Princess Diana photographs by Tim Graham ; doll photo courtesy of GATCO / Page 54 Photos courtesy of Hasbro's Sindy's Emanuel clothing box / Page 55 Photos courtesy of Hasbro's Naomi Campbell box and Matchbox's Beverly Johnson box / Pages 56-57 Photos and images courtesy of Galoob / Page 58 Photos by Beauregard Houston-Montgomery / Pages 59-62 Photos and sketches courtesy of Franklin Mint ; photo of Jackie Kennedy courtesy of JFK Library / Page 63 Pages from Tina Cassini's fashion booklet courtesy of Polly & Pam Judd / Page 64 Photo by Ande' Whyland / Page 65 Jacqueline doll with jewel case and photo of fashion sketch by Ande' Whyland ; photo of Jacqueline Onassis by Beauregard Houston-Montgomery; other photos courtesy of Alexander Doll Company / Page 67 Sketch by Bob Mackie courtesy of Mattel / Page 68 Photograph by Beauregard Houston-Montgomery, sketch courtesy of Franklin Mint / Page 69 Photo courtesy of Mattel; sketch and photo courtesy of Mego / Page 70 Photo courtesy of Mattel / Page 71 Photo by John Kisch / Pages72-73 Photos courtesy of Mattel, Franklin Mint / Page 74 Photo by Beauregard Houston-Montgomery / Pages 75-77 Photo of Audrey Hepburn in Funny Face courtesy of Paramount Pictures; all other photos courtesy of Mattel / Pages78-79 Photos courtesy of Knickerbocker Co., Franklin Mint , and Alexander Doll Company / Page 80 Photos of Gene and Mel Odom by TImothy Greenfield-Sanders / Pages 81-83 "Blonde Lace" pantsuit photo by Gene Bagnato; all other photos courtesy of Ashton-Drake / Pages 84-85 Photos of Cindy Adams and boxed doll by Timothy Greenfield-Sanders; doll photos by Laura Meisner / Page 86 Photo by Beauregard Houston-Montgomery; Barbie photo courtesy of Mattel / Pages 87-93 Photos courtesy of Mattel / Page 94 Sketch of Billyboy by Clyde Smith / Page 95 Sketch of Theatre of Fashion Barbie by Rene Gruau; both sketches courtesy of Mattel / Page 97 Photos courtesy of Billyboy ; sketch by Clyde Smith / Page 98 Photos courtesy of Mattel / Page 99 Photos courtesy of Alexander Doll Company / Pages 100-101 Photos by Beauregard Houston-Montgomery ; sketches by Jennifer Anderson / Page 102 Photo of John Mckitterick by Ande' Whyland; photo courtesy of Totem Intl. / Page 103 Photo of Billy in Paul Smith by Beauregard Houston-Montgomery; photos and sketch courtesy of Totem, Intl. / Page 104 Photo of Audrey Hepburn in "Funny Face" courtesy of Paramount Pictures ; sketch courtesy of Mattel / Page 105 Photos courtesy of Ashton-Drake, Alexander Doll Co.; Barbie trading card courtesy of Mattel / Page 106 Photos courtesy of Ashton-Drake, Mattel, Knickerbocker Co; photo of Miss Seventeen by Ande' Whyland ; gown by Phyllis Belanger; sketch courtesy of Mattel / Page 107 Photos courtesy of Alexander Doll Co., Ashton-Drake, Mattel, Knickerbocker Co. / Page 108 Photos courtesy of Mattel, Ashton Drake; sketch courtesy of Billyboy / Page 109 Photos courtesy of Ashton Drake, Totem, Intl.; photo of Bradford Samuels doll by Kevin Mulligan; sketch courtesy of Mattel / Page 110 Photo of Bradford Samuels by Alan Purcell / Pages 111-13 Photos by Kevin Mulligan / Page 114 Photo courtesy of Alexander Doll Company / Page 115 Photos courtesy of Alexander Doll Company, Ashton Drake / Page 116 Photos courtesy of Ashton Drake / Page 117 Sketches courtesy of Louis Marx & Company, Mattel, Billyboy / Pages 118-19 Sketches courtesy of Mattel, Louis Marx & Co., and John Puzewski / Pages 120-125 Photos courtesy of Alexander Doll Company, Mattel, Ashton Drake, and Franklin Mint / Page 122 Photo by Steven Mays / Page127 Photo by Beauregard Houston-Montgomery / Page 128 Photo by Benita Cassar Torreggiani / Back Cover Photo of Bradford Samuel's Chanel-Inspired Doll by Kevin Mulligan.

ABOUT THE
AUTHOR

Beauregard Houston-Montgomery has written for a wide variety of magazines including *Vogue, Harper's Bazaar, Vanity Fair, World of Interiors, Elle, Elle Decor, Interview, Details,* and *Playgirl.* His doll writing has appeared in *Family Circle, Doll Journal, Contemporary Doll, Doll Reader®, Dolls,* and *BARBIE® Magazine.* Previous books include *Pouf Pieces* (Hanuman Books), as well as contributions to *Dog People* (Artisan Books), and an upcoming tome on entertaining due out next year by Brigid Berlin. The author resides in New York City.